# OPENING *into* WORSHIP

# OPENING *into* WORSHIP

*Discovering how each book
of the Bible opens into worship*

L. Diane Forsyth

Library of Congress Control Number: 2005929763

The suggested Library of Congress subject heading for this book is:
Worship in the Bible.


© 2005 Charistis
A Ministry Dedicated to Spiritual Life Development of Adults and Children.

PO Box 4828, Pasco WA 99302

www.charistis.org

ISBN-13: 978-0-9769147-1-6
ISBN-10: 0-9769147-1-9

 WHITESTONE PRESS

415 N. Quay St., Suite A6, Kennewick WA 99336

*This book is*
*consecrated*
*to God*
*Who created us*
*to worship*
*and*
*it is*
*dedicated*
*to all*
*who are*
*opening into worship.*

# About the cover

*Water and fire*
*are irreconcilable elements.*
*Aren't they?*
*They extinguish each other.*
*Don't they?*

*Human and divine*
*have as much hope of*
*uniting*
*as do water and flame.*
*Don't they?*

*Yet*
*in Christ*
*water and fire*
*unite.*
*The Water[1] and*
*the Fire[2]*
*complement each other.*
*Coming together*
*they surround us in a mystery*
*that opens us to worship.*

*In Christ*
*human and divine are*
*forever united.*
*Living this union*
*we open always more fully into worship.*

---

[1] "And I heard, as it were, the voice of a great multitude and as the sound of many waters and as the sound of mighty peals of thunder, saying, Hallelujah! For the Lord our God, the Almighty, reigns." Revelation 19:6, NASB. Fresh waters flow into the sea's hallelujah, and from there, evaporation, clouds, rain, springs and rivers give life again as they return to the sea's hallelujah. Regarding the water, see also Psalm 93:4, NIV; John 3:5, 4:10-11, 7:37-38; Revelation 1:15, 21:6, 22:1,17.

[2] Regarding the fire, see Exodus 3:1-5; Deuteronomy 4:24; Luke 12:49; Acts 2:3,4; 2 Timothy 1:6, NIV; Hebrews 12:29.

# Acknowledgments

A book is not a solo flight. Certainly not this one, anyway! Yes, there is an author, but she is not the only reason you are holding this book in your hands.

Danny next door, Hittles in California, Jeannette in Massachusetts, Dennis right here in the Tri-Cities and others in the United States and beyond have helped this book happen.

"Danny, I would love to paint with you now, but I'm…" "You're working, aren't you?" "Yes, Danny, I'm working on the book. Thank you so much for coming, but I can't play now." For Danny, his brother Giovanni, and all my young neighbor friends, including Leslie and Sofia who have moved, and whom I keep missing, a big thank-you for all the fun we have had together drawing, painting, reading, flying paper airplanes and just talking. During the year and a half that I've been working on this book I would have liked to give you more time, but instead I'm giving you this book. You may not know what to do with it yet. But the time will come when you will be able to recognize it as a very big "I love you" from me, and most of all, from God.

Alix and Lauryn, my great nieces, thank you too, and for similar reasons. You live too far away to knock on our door very often, but we could have come to your birthday parties last year, except I stayed home those two weekends to work on this book. Thank you for the fun we have had making clay animals, tissue flowers and chasing bubbles or whirling football frisbees, and for walks and talks. This book is another "I love you;" it's for you when the time is right. The Love it's about has been, and will always be, yours.

Ted, Debbie, Brittany and Joshua Hittle and Barbara, your years of sustained support for Charistis have made more difference than any of us realize yet. May you, and the others who have given to Charistis, know how much this book, and its life, is also yours.

Thank you, Rich Breshears, Kaarina Makowski, and Julie Dewberry for your much-appreciated help through the months of discovering just where and how this book would be designed and published.

Dennis Miller, someone had to finish what had been mulled over for months! You and your staff did that. You designed, formatted and printed it, with a special kind of regard for its content and its author. Thank you for that regard, and thanks so much for being great to work with. I'm glad you will continue to be there in behalf of this book's future.

Russ Reddinger, to whom I report in my job at Duratek, thank you. You are the kind of manager who helps make it possible to be and do what a person is meant to be and do, including this book.

Jeannette Cézanne, after networking, e-mails to many potential editors, phone conversations, prayer and providence, you became this book's editor. Thank you. Thank God. I like your e-mails, Jeannette! They are simple, clear, and encouraging. You make being edited bearable, even pleasant. That's not all. You are in touch with the things that matter even more than the millions of details. Thank you for appreciating and sharing in the heart of this book.

Things that matter most to me, like this book and all that has led up to it, always remind me of how much I appreciate my family. Love from and for my family has deeply influenced this book. Thank you. I love you.

The one who has seen this book at the closest range, whose middle name is Patience, my husband, Robert, thank you. You have waited, watched, and worked with me. You led me to Rich who led us to Dennis. You've checked information, written permission letters, and verified every one of a thousand (more or less) footnotes. In fact, you've even read every word of the manuscript! Thank you for loving *Opening Into Worship* and me. Thank you, also, to your understanding, accepting family whose loving support is a great blessing in my life.

Those who came to the consecration service for this book, and those who wanted to, thank you. It is consecrated to the One I thank most of all. Like my Brother Jesus, I am not alone, my Father is with me. He is the One who gives this book its life and future. A

# Contents

# Introduction

This book explores how each book of the Bible opens into worship, and how *we* open into worship. It asks for a theology of worship that is based on this opening into worship.

I hope you, the one reading these words, will love and enter into worship all the more because of this book.

I would like you to know how much this is a part of me. Before I was born, I began attending worship services with my three older brothers and our daddy and mother. One October day I joined them—a crying baby who had to be carried out during the worship service! The roots of this book, therefore, go deep. And from the roots of my life grows a love of worship that is bound for eternity. I want you to know that this book comes out of a lifetime of loving God.

I want you to know so much more than that. I want you to know always more fully the longing and reverence that draw us into worship. I want you to experience this reverence and longing for worship as the hungers they are, hungers that are always being satisfied, and always being renewed.

Most of all I want you to know—always more fully—the Only One who makes worship happen. We can want it and do our best to prepare for it, but in the end worship is a gift. I want you to receive the gift of worship, and receive it often.

If through this book you are blessed and drawn to love and enter into worship all the more, then it has accomplished its purpose. And you and I can thank God.

The desire to worship, and not just attend church, has been getting stronger and stronger in my life for a long time. I believe this is so for other people also. I came to a place where I wanted to do more than hear words about God at church. I wanted to encounter

God and respond to Him with appropriate reverence and worship. Hearing sermons or reading articles about being a traditional or contemporary worshipper did nothing to satisfy this desire. Although I didn't want to continue reading this or that article, about this or that worship style, it did occur to me that knowing what the Bible says about worship would help. What *do* I believe, what *do* Adventists believe about worship? Do we have a theology of worship? What substantial biblical studies have Adventists done about worship? Have we done more than gather some Bible texts together about one or more aspects of worship? If you are not a Seventh-day Adventist, please read on anyway. This book is for you too.

I began to look. In the book *Seventh-day Adventists Believe...*[1] I found incidental mention of worship on three pages, but no doctrine about it. I received gracious help from some Adventist pastors and teachers who are acquainted with the resources about this subject, but even they said that there are few published sources about worship by Adventists. They directed me to two or three books, and to some articles in church papers. Most of the articles have to do with application—for example, questions of worship style. Not many have to do with substantial biblical studies or a theology of worship. There is one book, however, that goes beyond application. It was written in 1967 by the father of a friend of mine and is titled *And Worship Him*. In this book, Dr. Norval Pease, then Professor of Church and Ministry at the Andrews University Seminary, said, "We [Adventists] have published hundreds of books on the day of worship, but I don't know of one single Adventist book on the way of worship."[2] When I read that, I felt an ache something like he must have felt when he wrote it. Only now this shared ache is thirty-five years stronger.

This ache pressed into my being at a time when I was in an extended period of recovery from deeply exhausting grief after a death in the family. That grief was complicated by many years of circumstances that had kept my heart in hiding. With patience, prayer, and the help of a remarkable friend, heart-healing began for me. This continues, and I find heart-healing makes a life-giving difference in communion with God, including receiving God's word through Scripture. The people of God in every century have known how vitally important heart is; but some of us have to learn it, sometimes slowly.

This book is meant to be from heart and to heart, from the heart of the writer to the hearts of the recipients. I use the word heart in both of the ways I find it used in the Bible. Sometimes I find it refers to one aspect of our being, usually the one that pertains to feeling or emotion (as opposed to sentimentalism). Other times — the majority of times — I find Scripture uses the word heart to describe the center of our whole being. In this broader, fuller sense, heart includes the capacity to receive and respond with feeling, the capacity to reason, and other capacities as well. In the second and full sense, the word heart draws us into wholeness and balance. Heart is the place in us where every aspect of our being converges, with no aspect dominating and no aspect hiding.

Heartwork is a term I use in this book to describe a prayerful commitment to a healthy heart in the fullest biblical sense of the word. I, as well as others, have often prayed in a way that enlists the help of the Spirit of God in thinking through the words of Scripture and coming to a logical conclusion. In heartwork my prayer expands, and I become intentional about more than processing words. I pray that God will enable me to receive His Word in the center of my whole being, where all aspects of my being can respond, in the Spirit as God wills. This heartwork honors the rational process, but also calls for so much more. One of the ways I experience God's merciful response to my heartwork is through a mingling of tears, insights, and meaning. Another, and more ultimate way, is in the sense of receiving more than I could come up with on my own. Flesh and blood has not revealed the things of God to us; neither has the most whole and balanced heart revealed them. The Spirit of God has. A healthy heart is just the best hospitality I can offer to the Spirit.

When I didn't find an Adventist theology of worship, I was all the more convinced of the need for it. One day it became clear what I needed to do. It became as clear as any assignment (and more clear than many assignments!) I've received in school or on the job: Find out if or how each book of the Bible opens into worship. Write a book about what you find. Offer it to those who might expand it into a theology of worship, or find a way for this to be done. Offer it also to anyone who loves, or wants to love, worship—whether or not they are an Adventist, and whether or not they do anything more with it than read it and be blessed by it. In other words, this book that asks Adventists to develop a theology of worship is also for anyone interested in what the Bible reveals about worship.

I started at Genesis and worked straight through the Bible. With each Scriptural book I entered into the heartwork I described above. Then I read one or two brief introductions to each book. Then I checked for some of the same worship-related words in each book. Then I wrote about the opening or openings into worship that I found in each book. I spent about five months using *Young's Analytical Concordance* before changing to an online concordance. The King James Version that Young's is based on remained the predominant version I used. When other versions are quoted in this book, they are noted.

My desire and hope for this book soar, but when confined to words in this introduction, they become like a bird on foot. However, by the mercy of God and the ministry of the Spirit, you can mount up with wings as you read, ponder and respond to *Opening Into Worship. /*

Laurita Diane Forsyth

---

[1] Ministerial Association, 1988, *Seventh-day Adventists Believe... A Biblical Exposition of 27 Fundamental Doctrines*, Ministerial Association, General Conference of Seventh-day Adventists, Silver Spring, Maryland.

[2] Since Dr. Pease wrote this, two related books have been published: Raymond Holmes, *Sing a New Song: Worship Renewal for Adventists Today*, Andrews University Press, Berrien Springs, Michigan, 1984, and Pedrito U. Maynard-Reid, *Diverse Worship: African-American, Caribbean & Hispanic Perspectives* is a book by an Adventist author and published by Intervarsity Press, Downers Grove, Illinois, 2000.

# Heartwork

Heartwork is not analysis. Not scholarship. Not sentimentalism. It's neither heady nor touchy-feely, as advocates of two extremes tend to describe each other. The written consequences of heartwork can't be filed within either academic literature or devotional literature. And heartwork writing can't be filed in the general category of spirituality that includes free-floating writings that are, too often, disconnected from Bible, Gospel and Church. There are a lot of things that heartwork is not. But what about what it *is*?

In order to understand heartwork better, consider a blueberry. How many nutrients, phytochemicals, antioxidants, and other life-sustaining elements are present in a blueberry? Even those who are well trained in figuring out such things say they have not all been identified yet. In other words, we still don't really know exactly what a blueberry is. Humans have labeled some of the powerful parts of a blueberry, and they know enough to stand back and say that we can never duplicate its full being.

A human being is at least as complex, and amazing, as a blueberry. How many aspects (also known as faculties) are there in a human being? In response to that question, Deuteronomy 6, Matthew 12, Luke 10, and even more contemporary sources—such as the Walla Walla College seal—may come to mind. All of these, and so many more sources, contribute labels such as: heart, soul, might, mind, strength, physical, mental, social, emotional, body, spirit, and more. There are a lot of labels for various aspects of our being. And there is a lot of discussion about which labels mean approximately the same thing, and which labels are subordinate to which, and which arrangement of labels, or paradigm, is best and why. Things like that. But do we know *all* a human being is? I doubt it. Not when we still don't even know what a blueberry is.

Our good health, and with it our happiness, is served by loving and respecting the whole blueberry. I receive the blueberry, appreciating all I can know about it, and respecting the much more I don't know about it. I let the whole blueberry nourish and satisfy me —and taste so good in the process!

Heartwork honors and benefits from wholeness at least as much as, and in fact much more than that! In heartwork I appreciate what I can know about being human, and I also respect all that I don't know about it. My Heart is the place where every aspect of my being converges or originates. I know, or at least have labels for, some of these aspects, but not for all of them. In heartwork, I receive the Word and Spirit of God into my Heart where every aspect of my being can engage the Word and the Spirit according to that aspect's ability. Thinking (reasoning) and feeling (emoting) are two dominant and often conflicting aspects. It is too possible to let one, or both, claim more than its share. When I do that, heartwork is crippled, or divided. Healthy heartwork honors all aspects. Sometimes I just need to sit still with the Word and the Spirit, and let heartwork be what God is making of it.

Heartwork intentionally takes me into wholeness. Heartwork also takes me into the place where potency and potential are maximized. Consider the heart of a kernel, known as the germ. Consider the small sprout of a seed where every element is concentrated. Consider how literally life-giving and life-engaging this heart of the grain is, this heart of the whole plant. Heartwork involves literally receiving and engaging life in the place of its greatest potency and potential.

Heartwork also involves tears. Tears vary enormously in what they express, and how they affect the one who cries and those nearby. Chemically, even, tears vary according to what prompts them. These are facts about tears that can be verified by observation and science. There is more. This something more can be verified by participation: the tears that come with Spirit-guided heartwork express something more soft and more solid than any other tears. These tears don't signal weakness; instead they show that a person is entering into his or her greatest strength. Those who develop a

theology of anything, certainly a theology of worship, need to
excel in tears as surely as, or even more surely than, they excel in
scholarship.

It's not easy to excel in tears. It's harder yet to show others the
way. And how would a person measure the results? There are tests
to measure one's intelligence quotient, or I.Q. Is there any measure
of tears, the tears that go beyond emotionalism or sentimentalism?
Of course not. And yet there are indicators. For one thing, there is
an authenticity, even authority, in the words (written or spoken)
of a person who excels in tears. If there were such a thing as T.Q.
(tear quotient) it might reflect how much a person cries—or it might
reflect a person's capacity for depth or intensity of grief and joy.
Heartwork takes us into always new depths and heights of grief
and joy.

One way to summarize Heartwork might be the dynamic by
which our whole being receives and responds to the Word and Spirit
of God. Heartwork is the best hospitality we can offer to the Spirit of
God, Who makes us soft and strong in the fear and love of God. *H*

# Genesis

"Abraham was now old and well advanced in years, and the LORD had blessed him in every way."[1] So begins one of the two chapters in Genesis that use the word *shachah*, which means to bow self down, to worship.

The strength of his blessings, the vulnerability of his age, the wisdom and humility of his faith are all expressed and multiplied in this chapter. The recent death of Sarah, the future of Isaac and his descendants, the strength of family (his own family of origin, and the family he anticipates for Isaac), the greater-yet strength of God's providence and promises—all of these pack each word and gesture of this chapter with heart and meaning. So much converges as Abraham says to the chief servant in his household, the one in charge of all that he has, "Put your hand under my thigh. I want you to swear by the LORD, the God of heaven and the God of earth, that you will not get a wife for my son from the daughters of the Canaanites, among whom I am living, but will go to my country and my own relatives and get a wife for my son Isaac."[2] And, "make sure that you do not take my son back there."[3]

Through tests failed and tests passed, Abraham's faith had been purified over and over. Now it was on the line again, and with it, the power of Sarah's and his love for Isaac. Led by God, Abraham had responded with faith and had made a new life in a new country. But the love and significance of his family of origin was never lost. Only God's providence and promises mattered more to Abraham. Now all of this, everything that mattered most, was on the line as Abraham

sent his servant to find a wife for Isaac. Abraham sent his assurance
with his servant: "The God of heaven will send his angel before you."

After swearing the oath, the servant took all kinds of good things
with him and set out for Nahor. Near the well, outside the town,
he prayed, "O LORD, God of my master Abraham, give me success today, and show kindness to my master Abraham." Then he
described how he would know the answer to his prayer.[4]

Rebekah, who was very beautiful and equally hospitable and gracious, came and fulfilled the sign. "Then the man bowed down and
worshiped the LORD."[5]

All Abraham's age with its accumulation of wisdom, love,
faith, humility and hope—all of this; and

All the yearning for Isaac's happiness and well-being, and the
same yearning for the well-being of all Isaac's future family; and

All the strength of what Abraham's family meant to him and
what it meant to be the son of his father and mother; and

All the greater-yet strength of God's providence and promises
that sent Abraham away from his family of origin into a pilgrim-
age of faith;

*All of this* reaches a grand crescendo. It must be expressed,
must be released, and it is—in worship.

Then worship moved the servant, Abraham's spokesman, forward to dialogue with Rebekah's family. Everything unspoken that
comes to this chapter, and everything said and done in the chapter,
culminates in worship—worship that, in turn, inspires, or perhaps
only makes bearable, the sudden parting between Rebekah and her
mother, and brother: her home.

Worship such as this is like the breaking of a great ocean wave.
There's a lot of movement as the wave swells, gains momentum, then
breaks; and there's a lot of movement as it flows on after it breaks.
In the movement and events of Abraham's and his servant's days, a
wave of worship would begin to swell. Through their communion
with God, this wave gained momentum, until in some moment either
alone or with other people of God, the wave broke into worship.
Satisfied and rejuvenated by worship, they moved back into ordinary
daily events and communion with God that would then move and

culminate in worship once again.

The might and splendor of realized worship (the crash of the wave) is not isolated from the cresting before, and the subsiding after, the wave breaks. Life fully lived in communion and promise and in ever-refined and expanding faith and humility will repeatedly crescendo into worship, and from there flow on to the next crescendo of worship. A theology of worship will help us know—will help us actually experience—both the momentum-building life with God and the worship into which it will break. It will show us how daily communion with God and the crescendos of worship serve and sustain each other. *G*

[1] Genesis 24:1, NIV

[2] Genesis 24:3-4, NIV

[3] Genesis 24:6, NIV

[4] Genesis 24:12-14, NIV

[5] Genesis 24:26, NIV

# Exodus

The manifest, visible presence of Yahweh is at the heart of worship in Exodus. In response, the people bowed low and worshipped. This happened when the sons of Israel realized Yahweh was concerned about them and had seen their affliction.[1] Their worship at that point demonstrated both heart and courage in worship. Heart, because it flowed from awareness of Yahweh's compassionate concern, and courage, because this experience in worship served to arm them for seeing the plagues that followed.

The people also bowed low and worshipped when they heard the meaning of the Passover.[2] This came at the end of the plagues and just before the Exodus began. It was a time when God's protection of His people and God's judgment against Pharaoh and Pharaoh's people were vivid and real to them. Worship happens in the face of both: God's enormous mercy and also God's terrifying judgments.

Worship occurred at pivotal moments such as these. In addition, whenever they saw the pillar of cloud standing at the entrance of the tent of meeting, "all the people would arise and worship, each at the entrance of his tent."[3]

"Moses made haste to bow low toward the earth and worship" when Yahweh had passed by in front of him and proclaimed His character.[4] Worship resulted from words about God; words expressed by God Himself. Imagine God wanting you to know Him; God telling you about himself! When that happened to Moses, he bowed low toward the earth and worshipped.

A theology of worship will renew our heart's desire for the

manifest, visible presence of God. It will also train us in a response that is full of heart and holy fear and that bows low in worship.

There's more in Exodus. It's incredibly rich with worship. It is Exodus that shows us worship as hospitality. God wants the hospitality of His people. Prepare a place for Me, I want to come and be with you.[5] A theology of worship will help us live into the difference between worship as hospitality and worship as some of the other things it seems to become. It will show us, more and more, what is involved in honoring and receiving the One who desires our hospitality. This is a different kind of movement than that which is commonly associated with worship services.

There were many parts and pieces involved in preparing the place! So many. Many people and many skills brought all these parts and pieces together, and it was beautiful—a true labor of love done as they were told to do it. Individuals had crafted beautiful items. These were deeply significant (especially to the one whose labor of love they were), yet these individual items became a small part of the combined, splendid offering of the sanctuary, which in turn was dwarfed by the glorious presence of God that filled it. There was a succession of surpassing splendor, with compounding significance. The end was worship, a reward beyond words. A theology of worship will show us the way of individual and corporate preparation for receiving the One who comes in the ultimate surpassing splendor that reduces us all to the unspeakable joy of worship.

The book of Exodus ends with this:

> *Throughout all their journeys, the cloud of the LORD was on the tabernacle by day, and there was fire in it by night, in the sight of all the house of Israel.*[6]

A theology of worship will help us take in the compassion and comfort of this heart-full summation. Worship was so visible, so central, so connected with all of life. It is so good. So very good. *E*

---

[1] Exodus 4:31      [4] Exodus 34:6-8, NASB

[2] Exodus 12:27      [5] Exodus 25:8

[3] Exodus 33:10, NASB      [6] Exodus 40:38, NASB

# Leviticus

Atonement is at the heart of Leviticus and it is the way that Leviticus opens into worship. On the Day of Atonement, Israelites came closest to the Holy God... who was always in the midst of them.

> *...in the seventh month, on the tenth day of the month, you shall humble your souls, and not do any work...it is on this day that atonement shall be made for you to cleanse you; you shall be clean from all your sins before the LORD. It is to be a sabbath of solemn rest for you, that you may humble your souls.*[1]

At the heart of Leviticus, atonement. At the heart of atonement, humbling of soul. Through humbling their souls, they received atonement. In this they realized, actually lived into, being holy as God is holy. God told them repeatedly, "Be holy for I am holy."[2]

On the Day of Atonement they were to approach the Holy God who was always in the midst of them. They were to come close with the greatest care. The priest was to exactly follow atonement instructions in every detail. The people were to do one thing, and do it well: Humble your souls.

A theology of worship will show us the timeless truth that humbling our souls is essential in order to come close to our Holy God. A theology of worship will light the way, helping us do it, not just discuss it.

The altar was, surely, a most profound way into humility of soul for the faithful people of God. The word altar slides easily into religious conversation. The term "slaughter place" does not. Yet the Hebrew word *mizbeach*, that is translated altar, means slaughter place. Leviticus has eighty-two references to *mizbeach*. It can't be easily avoided. Leviticus also has eighty-seven references to holy. Holy is from *qadosh or qodesh*, and is about being separate and set apart.

The *mizbeach* was not a common or secular place. It was a holy altar. That doesn't remove the abhorrent element in the picture, but it does drastically change the picture. All of the unthinkable slaughter that happened at the altar was holy. It takes a humble soul to see and accept this holy mystery of the *mizbeach* for what it is.

*The life of the flesh is in the blood, and I have given it to you on the altar to make atonement for your souls; for it is the blood by reason of the life that makes atonement.*[3]

People who participated, and certainly people who read about it centuries later, could respond in various ways ranging from being repulsed to being indifferent. What a terrible, barbaric thing some thought. The heathen do things like that, but *our* God doesn't ask it of us. He is too good and compassionate to allow such slaughter. Others, through repeatedly seeing it, or hearing of it, became immune or indifferent.

However, when they humbled their souls they were no longer repulsed or indifferent. Humbling of soul took them past heart-hardening, past blocking, and into the pain and peace of the holy slaughter place.

A theology of worship will show us the way past heart-hardening, past blocking, and into the pain and peace of the Cross. Humbling of soul takes us into—actually into—the deepest of all grief and also into the most holy joy. A theology of worship may show us how to read, preach, sing and pray about it; but more than that, it will enable us to do it—to simply, actually humble our souls. *L*

[1] Leviticus 16:29-31, NASB
[2] Leviticus 11:44,45; 19:2; 20:7,26; 21:6,8, NASB
[3] Leviticus 17:11, NASB

# Numbers

When the cloud by day and pillar of fire by night remained over the sanctuary, the Israelites camped behind, beside, and before it. When the cloud and pillar of fire moved, the Israelites "set forward" with the sanctuary.

> *Thou, O LORD, art in the midst of this people, for Thou, O LORD, art seen eye to eye, while Thy cloud stands over them; and Thou dost go before them in a pillar of cloud by day and in a pillar of fire by night.[1]*

What an encampment! With the visible presence of God right there in the center, they set up their tents on every side and facing it. Their hearts were drawn and cautioned by the Holy God in their midst.

> *And whenever the cloud was lifted from over the tent, afterward the sons of Israel would then set out; and in the place where the cloud settled down, there the sons of Israel would camp.[2]*

The dismantling and moving of the sanctuary and all its contents was a literal, hands-on experience with holy things. It should be noted, however, that it wasn't hands-on for everyone. Some were not to touch the holy things. Aaron and his sons covered the holy objects and all the furnishings of the sanctuary. After that, the sons of Kohath carried them, so that they would not touch the holy objects and die.[3] Dismantling, moving, and re-assembling all involved a keen sense of the holy.

This was similar, and is also exactly opposite to the situation at the Hanford Site in Washington State, where there is constant mindfulness about radiological contamination. Radiation and its damaging, death-dealing effects are always on everyone's mind at Hanford, where nuclear waste is processed and stored. In Israel, I can imagine, there was a similar mindfulness about holiness, because in Israel there were rules for exactly how to handle holy things, just as there are regulations for just how to handle radiation-exposed things at Hanford. As at Hanford, so in Israel, people were made aware and kept aware: you don't trifle with this. It's a matter of life and death.

On the other hand, in Israel the situation was exactly opposite to that at Hanford, because holy things were at the center of their *life* as a people. Yes, a person could die if holy objects were handled inappropriately. But the holy objects were life-charged; they were not death-dealing, radiation-contaminated objects.

In Israel, and at Hanford, awareness was and is crucial. It was, and is, aroused and forever renewed. At Hanford, the people are aware, they conform, and beyond that they may be irritated or thankful that they never stop hearing about the dangers of radiation. In Israel, the people were aware and they conformed—or they rebelled, and died.

Beyond that there is a magnificent difference because of how the people of Israel were, or at least had the choice to be, affected by the holy objects they dismantled, transported, and reassembled. Each person who had a part in moving, if not actually touching, the holy objects, held a piece of the dwelling place of God in his hands. How much were they taken into that awareness, and what heart response did it create in them? I don't know, but I believe the answer has a lot to do with how they entered into the humbling of soul on the Day of Atonement. And how they lived into that humbling, day-by-day, between the annual days of atonement. Humbling of soul brought them close and kept them close to the One whose glory filled the sanctuary. With a heart tuned by humility, a person could be deeply moved by holding a part of God's dwelling place in his hands.

Holiness and worship go together. How do we become aware of the holy? How do we learn to handle what is holy? How do we learn to respect and love the holy? A theology of worship will ponder these things. It will tune our eyes, ears, and hearts to the holy. It will contribute to ever-deepening reverence in response to the holy. N

[1] Numbers 14:14, NASB
[2] Number 9:17, NASB
[3] Numbers 4:15, NASB

# Deuteronomy

Deuteronomy uses the word "command" seventy-seven times. It uses the word "commandment" forty-two times. These and related words are what we might call the *high use* words in Deuteronomy. The New American Standard Bible says that Deuteronomy means *repetition of the law*. The book is full of appeals to keep the law. It is full of dire outcomes to Israel if it does not obey. There are horrifying curses and drastic, torturing outcomes. The emphasis on law, punishment, and curses might take a reader of Deuteronomy further and further away from thoughts about or inclination to worship. It might; but it must not. Fear the LORD thy God. Love the LORD thy God. These are deeper and higher than everything else Deuteronomy commands Israel to do and be. The reason Israel was commanded to hear God's words[1] and to hear and keep all of God's commandments[2] was so that the people of Israel would learn to fear the LORD their God, the name that is glorious and fearful.[3] Everything in Deuteronomy pointed them to fear and love God.

God's people (Israel then, us now) keep missing the point. It is so obvious, yet becomes strangely illusive. God would not have given one law, not a statute, not a precept, not a testimony, not a commandment, that wasn't a pointer. He would not have given a law that didn't teach His people to fear and love Him. You shall love the LORD your God with all your heart, soul, and might,[4] and here is how you do it. Then comes another command. Command after command, the whole book of them, is about loving the LORD your God with all your heart, soul, and might. When God's people focus on the command itself, it no longer serves as a pointer, and the curse begins. When God's people obey the commands, following them where they point, the blessing begins and continues. When the fear and love of God are actively increasing, worship is happening, or certainly will happen.

A theology of worship will keep the blessing of law bound up with the experience of worship. It won't give us one without the other. And a theology of worship will always focus where worship can only focus, which is on this glorious and fearful name: THE LORD THY GOD.[5] To do this we will need to be "schooled"—not so much by theories as by experience—in the fear of God. A theology of worship will show us the fear of God, a holy fear that is reverence and more.

Near the end of Deuteronomy, in chapters 31 and 32, there is a compelling opening into worship that turns worship, as we think of it, upside down. In these chapters, God is singing to His people. Don't many people, especially in what is called contemporary worship, think of worship as singing praise songs to God? But this is God singing to Israel. And it isn't praise. It's a ballad; more than that, it's a love song, a love song about infidelity, about Israel breaking the covenant, turning to other gods and serving them. And it's a song about Love that's bigger than their unthinkable infidelity. "The LORD will have compassion on His servants . . .[6] And will atone for His land and His people."[7] Those are the last words of the song. The broken-hearted Lover triumphs. This is not lovesick sentimentalism; this is the heart of God being trampled on, and *still refusing to leave.* It's about divine love going deeper and extending way higher than Israel's covenant-keeping and covenant-breaking. This opening into worship shows the hard, heart-breaking realities of broken covenant that so decimate the people of God and so crush the heart of God. It *never* should have been this way, *never* should have come out this way, but it did. After the worst possible outcomes materialize, and suffering reigns everywhere in Israel and in the heart of God, then the surpassing expression of divine love comes, and it is vulnerable and strong so far beyond human comprehension:

*He will atone for His land and His people.*

Worship takes the worshipper into the hard places of broken covenant and suffering and also into the Love that triumphs through suffering. ⟁

[1] Deuteronomy 4:10

[2] Deuteronomy 8:6

[3] Deuteronomy 28:58

[4] Deuteronomy 6:5

[5] Deuteronomy 28:58

[6] Deuteronomy 32:36, NASB

[7] Deuteronomy 32:43, NASB

# Joshua

"And Joshua fell on his face to the earth, and did worship...."[1] Joshua's whole body responded, and not with knees bent, hands on the pew in front of him, forehead on knuckles. Instead, Joshua's face touched earth as his body responded to encounter with the captain of the LORD's host. All the worshippers I have seen, and the worshipper I have been, only approach the Bible's fullest worship posture. To some degree we put our body into worship; to some degree we actually encounter God as we do it. But we need so much compassion from each other, and most of all from God, as we approach fuller worship.

Joshua fell on his face to the earth because the actual face-to-face encounter had happened. We fall on our knees hoping it will. When faith, humility and longing are alive and becoming what they are meant to be, we *can* hope that worship will become what it, also, is meant to be.

Joshua also asked the captain of the LORD's host, " 'What has my lord to say to his servant?' And the captain of the LORD's host said to Joshua...." I thought about how we might complete that sentence, if we didn't know what he said. Based on other Scriptures, and on some "life commandments," I, for one, might complete that sentence with, "...take care of the widows and orphans," or "...keep God's commandments," or "...love your enemies." But none of those is what the captain of the LORD's host said to Joshua. Instead, he said, "Remove your sandals from your feet, for the place where you are standing is holy." And Joshua did so.[2] This opens into the heart of worship. Holiness is there. Worship will become what my heart, and God's heart, long for it to be when I see, and recognize, and respond appropriately to holiness. There *are* holy places, and they *do* get treated differently than ordinary places. Obedience to real encounter with God means really recognizing and responding to what is holy.

The worship at the end of chapter five comes at a crucial intersection, or point of transition, between homecoming and homemaking. At the end of chapter five, the Israelites have arrived in their new home. With chapter six they begin to make a home of it. Homemaking is gentle and comforting, isn't it? Battles are so utterly opposite to it. And yet, homemaking isn't just soft and gentle. Homemaking takes courage, strength and fortitude—things of battle. After their homecoming, Israel was in for some battle-ridden homemaking. The amazing thing is how God went with them into this battle-ridden homemaking. Where in the whole sanctuary complex was the closest of all to God? While they were pilgrims in the desert, the sanctuary was the heart of Israel's encampment. What was the heart of the sanctuary? The Ark. In the whole sanctuary complex, the Ark was the closest of all to God. The Ark was the most holy item of all, and it was placed in the most holy place of all, where only the high priest went, and only rarely. This one item at the heart of holiness was brought out and into battle. It is unthinkable. The most holy object from the sanctuary that summed up what worship was about going with Israel into battle. And doing it without being secularized. The Ark was no less holy on the battlefield than it was in the heart of the sanctuary. Its presence in the midst of battle shows that worshippers don't just go to a place of worship; worship goes with the worshipper into every part of life—including the hardest and worst parts. Worship is not just a sanctuary matter; it's an everyday, in the midst of the battle matter. A theology of worship will compassionately help us overcome our strange immunity and indifference to holiness. It will also help us be strengthened and comforted by the presence of worship and holiness in the midst of life's most difficult experiences.

[1] Joshua 5:14

[2] Joshua 5:14-15, NASB

# Judges

During the time of the Judges (about 300 years), Israel was homemaking, with all the clearing of the land and settling that involved. Throughout this book there isn't much emphasis on worship. As pilgrims in the desert, the sanctuary had been central to them. When they set up camp, their tents surrounded and faced the sanctuary. But there is no comparable picture recorded for the period of the judges. When they did build homes, were they purposefully positioned with reference to a house of worship? How long did they have homes before they replaced the temporary tent tabernacle with a permanent house of God? Judges shows Israelites clustered here and there throughout the land. During this period they were conquering sometimes, compromising other times. A cycle of apostasy-repentance-deliverance kept happening. I wonder how worship might have been experienced during those 300 years if that cycle had not been what it was? Had the rest of their life been better, how much better might their worship have been? Had their worship been better, how much better might the rest of their life have been?

Yet, in spite of all that, worship is included in Judges. And it is alive and essential. One introduction to Judges makes the point that the jealous and often bickering tribes of Israel were held together by their recognition of a common descent, and "still more by their common worship of the LORD."[1] Worship was the most binding, uniting factor in this 300 years. Even in the midst of these disruptive, turbulent times, worship was central. Their tents weren't all pitched in order around and facing the tabernacle anymore. But by now something in each of their tribes, each family, and each individual was as surely oriented to the dwelling place of God, and to worship. In spite of the cycle of apostasy-repentance-deliverance, worship was still the uniting, restoring center of their life as a unit, their life as God's people.

Although Judges doesn't say much about public worship, it does include worship. "When Gideon heard the dream, and its interpretation, he worshipped God."[2] This is another case of worship happening when a person came close to actual divine intervention. Like a human heart beats faster the closer lightning strikes; so worship happens more intensely the closer God comes. Worship is the pulse beat of our soul that is created for worship as literally and surely as our hearts are created to beat. Worship is activated and intensified by how close God is, that is how much we perceive God's closeness. The heart of worship is about coming cautiously close to the Fire and being warmed by it and having life sustained by it. This heart of worship has to do with deep respect and reverence for the Fire. Gideon, Joshua, and so many others before and after them knew this experience. They call us to the same kind of worship experience.

In various places the book of Judges mentions the altars and the house of God, and in this way repeatedly affirms the place of worship in the life its people. People that *were* a people because of worship. Yes, Judges opens into worship. Yet that worship is sadly affected by the cycle of apostasy-repentance-deliverance that characterized this troubled, tumultuous time. ⨉

[1] Introduction to Judges in *New American Standard Bible*, Cambridge Study Edition, Cambridge University Press, Cambridge, England.
[2] Judges 7:15, NIV

# Ruth

The book of Ruth opens into worship because of what it reveals about Ruth, who chose to worship God instead of the Moabite gods of her childhood. She left her own home, her own people, her own customs, and her own religion and chose to go with her mother-in-law saying, "Your people shall be my people, and your God, my God."[1]

When Boaz, the "mighty man of wealth" expressed his protective care for her, Ruth "fell on her face, and bowed herself to the ground, and said unto him, 'Why have I found grace in thine eyes...?' "[2] I can imagine Ruth bowed in respect to Boaz and in worship to God at the same time. Whether or not that was so, she expressed something that is at the heart of worship and contributes so much to worship: "Why have I found grace in thine eyes...?" It's so easy to come to God wondering why, with all His power, He isn't preventing suffering. When I can shift from that kind of wondering to Ruth's kind of wondering, it prepares me for worship.

As Boaz expressed his protective care for her, I can imagine Ruth was overcome by the impact of the moment, by how much converged there; her body expressed her response, and her heart recognized and gratefully received the grace in it. Doing this, Ruth mirrors the others (Moses, Joshua and all) who bowed in worship. Sadness, suffering, poverty, humility, gratitude, hope, these and more, converge in that moment. The same things are still at the heart of worship. As these things intensify, as we become more aware of them, the potential for significant worship intensifies. The strength and kindness

Ruth found in Boaz completely claimed and comforted her heart that was so fully aware of her sadness, suffering, poverty, and humility. Worship brings us, also, to encounter strength and kindness, God's grace, which completely claims and comforts our heart. Ruth was a woman with the heart capacity for realizing the enormity of her poverty and of grace. This same capacity opens us into worship.

Later in the story, Boaz is afraid (*charad* means "to tremble"),[3] and then he reassures Ruth saying "fear not" (*yare* not).[4] What Ruth had done, and what she was asking for, put so much on the line, and it opened into so much. Ruth must have only barely imagined how much. The *yare* response happens, or hovers ready to happen, when so much is on the line and the outcome could be glorious or disastrous. Ruth was a woman who courageously lived into such potential, and felt *yare* in the process! I'm sure she also felt the vastly larger *yare* in worshipful response to the God she chose.

A theology of worship will show us the way of the *yare* response in worship. It will also show us how to wonder, "Why have I found grace in your eyes, God?" ℛ

---

[1] Ruth 1:15,16, NASB
[2] Ruth 2:1,8-10
[3] Ruth 3:8
[4] Ruth 3:11

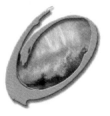

# 1 Samuel

The Ark of the Covenant was the physical, tangible heart of worship in Israel. Wherever the sanctuary (whether tent or temple) was, every part, every detail ultimately gathered around and supported the Ark. As the whole encampment of Israel surrounded and faced the tabernacle, so everything in the grounds and tabernacle surrounded and pointed to the Ark. There is no piece of furniture like it in church buildings today. The piece of furniture that claims the greatest respect in the most worshipful communities of faith still is not as charged as was the Ark with the actual presence of God.

In the sanctuary, this unapproachable, tangible heart of their worship was not visible, except once a year to one priest. Yet, this same tangible heart of worship that was kept intimately close, yet invisible and inaccessible, also went into battle with Israel's armies. From sanctuary shelter, where everything about the sanctuary and its services served reverence, the Ark went to war where exposure and vulnerability replaced shelter and reverence.

The book of 1 Samuel tells the unthinkable story of the Ark of God being taken by the Philistines.[1] The word that this happened brought on the death of the high priest and the birth of Ichabod. Birth this time spoke grief beyond our comprehension. The infant's widowed and dying mother named him Ichabod, saying, "The glory is departed from Israel: Because the Ark of God was taken...." Nothing is left but guilt, grief and the depths of abandonment. Ichabod's mother repeats, "The glory is departed from Israel: For the Ark of God is taken."[2] The light of their life as a people, and of each of them personally, was gone. The sun may as well not rise tomorrow.

When the Ark was in the land of the Philistines, it did not go well for their god Dagon or for their people; many of them died. As for Dagon, twice the Philistines found Dagon "fallen upon his face to the earth before the ark of the LORD."[3] An idol worshipping the LORD! Even the stones will cry out comes to mind.[4] What the Philistines made of Dagon was visibly surrendered to the LORD. Every knee shall bow to the one God of all![5] This also comes to mind. It's wonderful to have an idol so subordinated to the LORD. It answers that desire in us to have lightning strike the offenders. That part of the supernatural happenings associated with the Ark would have been good, even a great joy, to see. Many Philistines dying would not have been good to see. But that, also, was part of the happenings.

The Philistines tested to be sure these happenings were God's doings. They decided to send the Ark away on a cart pulled by two "milch kine." If it goes to Bethshemesh, they said, then the LORD has done us this great evil, but if not, then we will know it was a chance that happened to us. And the kine took the straight way to Bethshemesh. When the Philistines took the Ark into their town, into their house of Dagon, it precipitated events far beyond human accomplishment, including the death of many of their people.

The Israelites in Bethshemesh rejoiced to see the Ark. But, tragically, they also looked into the Ark of the LORD. As a result, thousands of them died. Then the Ark was moved to Kirjathjearim where it remained for twenty years while "all the house of Israel lamented after the LORD."[6]

When the Ark went into battle, very literal and concrete divine intervention happened. This was worship being worked out on the front lines where people were actually involved with the living God.

There are people in our culture today who are considered privileged, who use labels like primitive and superstitious to describe the kind of happenings recorded in 1 Samuel. They explain that since the Enlightenment and the Age of Reason, God doesn't have to deal with us like that any more. Before we unwittingly agree, we need to take it all very carefully to heart. Do we want to tame worship, retaining some intellectual and emotional meaning, but avoiding actual encounter with God? Our holy God is a consuming fire.[7] Yet there are Christian communities of faith who act as if He were only a refreshing drink of water. How does a worshipper know and respond to both the Fire and the Water? What is the timeless truth about worship in 1 Samuel 4 through 7? I'm sure it includes actual encounter with the Living God. Realizing that, I pray, "Forgive me, God, for insulating myself from significant encounter with You, and then being quietly, even condescendingly, superior about it. Forgive me for saying or thinking things like 'They couldn't help it; they were primitive, unlearned, and superstitious, but God loved them anyway.' Forgive me; forgive us, God. And, please satisfy this insatiable longing for You, God, that is not satisfied by words about You and to You. Let the heart of worship be taken into my heart, and take my heart into the heart of worship, please God."

A theology of worship will show us the way into full-fledged worship that does satisfy. ʃ

[1] 1 Samuel 4,5 and 6
[2] 1 Samuel 4:19-22
[3] 1 Samuel 5:3,4
[4] Luke 19:40
[5] Philippians 2:10
[6] 1 Samuel 7:1-2
[7] Hebrews 12:29

# 2 Samuel

David really wanted to build a house for God.[1] The book of 2 Samuel tells about this widely known desire of David's. It also tells about David bringing the Ark to Zion (the City of David).[2] And in the book's only two uses of the word worship, it shows David worshipping, each time in connection with deep grief over a son.[3]

This David, who is identified as a man after God's own heart,[4] shows us ever so much about how a person opens into worship. David is the author of a great many Psalms, and he also influenced many other Psalms. Worship is implicit and explicit throughout the 150 Psalms. Love for the house of God (the Psalms use various names for God's house) runs through the whole book of Psalms. The man after God's own heart *wanted to be there in the temple with God:*

> *But I, by your great mercy*
> *will come into your house;*
> *in reverence will I bow down*
> *toward your holy temple.*[5]
> ☞
>
> *One thing I ask of the LORD,*
> *this is what I seek:*
> *that I may dwell in the house of the LORD*
> *all the days of my life,*
> *to gaze upon the beauty of the LORD*
> *and to seek him in his temple.*[6]

⁀

*Within your temple, O God,*
 *we meditate on your unfailing love.*[7]

⁀

*Send forth your light and your truth,*
 *let them guide me;*
*let them bring me to your holy mountain,*
 *to the place where you dwell.*
*Then will I go to the altar of God,*
 *to God, my joy and my delight.*[8]

⁀

*Blessed are those you choose*
 *and bring near to live in your courts.*
*We are filled with the good things of your house,*
 *of your holy temple.*[9]

⁀

*Zeal for your house consumes me.*[10]

⁀

*How lovely is your dwelling place,*
 *O LORD Almighty!*
*My soul yearns, even faints,*
 *for the courts of the LORD;*
*my heart and my flesh cry out*
 *for the living God.*[11]

These and other Psalms portray David's heart for the place of worship and for being there with God. David leads the way in love of the place of worship and love of the acts of worship:

Reverently bowing down
Gazing upon the beauty of the LORD
Seeking God in his temple
Meditating on God's unfailing love
Delighting and rejoicing in God
Living in God's courts.

David, the man after God's own heart, loved the place of worship and was consumed with zeal for it. At the place of worship, the divine heart and the human heart found each other and spent "at home" time together.

It's this David, consumed with zeal for God's house, who brought the Ark of God from Baale-judah to Zion.[12] That is, it's this David — and 30,000 men of Israel who did. On the way, David took the Ark aside to the house of Obed-edom the Gittite where it stayed for three months. David did this because he was afraid to move the Ark into the city of David after Uzzah died (for taking hold of the Ark when the oxen shook it at Nachon's threshing-floor). Before they got to Nachon's threshing-floor, David and all the house of Israel played on "all manner of instruments made of fir wood, even on harps, and on psalteries, and on timbrels, and on cornets, and on cymbals."[13] Imagine this procession. The center, the very heart, of their place of worship was moving ahead of them. Music followed. Ah! To hear that music and to know what it expressed for this immense procession of people! And to know, with an insider's view, what this all meant to their king. How, in fact, did David's heart take it all in, and respond? Maybe there was a great variety in the music that expressed various aspects of heart and being. Maybe they sang about God's leading. There may have been songs of deliverance; songs of hope; songs of endurance; songs of repentance; and many more. How many of the Psalms we still know today might have been included then?

Then came the disaster at Nachon's threshing-floor: God's anger, Uzzah's death, David's displeasure and fear. This changed the destination of the Ark. David "carried it aside into the house of Obed-edom the Gittite."[14]

Three months later David heard that God blessed Obed-edom and his household because of the Ark. "So David went and brought up the Ark of God from the house of Obed-edom into the City of David with gladness."[15] When those who carried the Ark had gone six paces, David sacrificed oxen and fatlings. "And David danced before the LORD with all his might."[16] So David and all the house of Israel brought up the Ark of the LORD with shouting, and with the sound of the trumpet. When the Ark was set "in the midst of the tabernacle that David had pitched for it," David offered burnt offerings and peace offerings before the LORD.[17]

What mingling in the 2 Samuel 6 worship scene—from the heights (verse five) to the depths (verse seven) to the heights-higher-than-before (verses 14 and 15). The gladness and shouting mingled with confession and with death at the altar through sacrifices and offerings. The agility of David's soul is amazing. A very young child can send a smile and sparkling joy through eyes still wet from free-flowing tears. This may provide us with a glimpse of the deep, Spirit-filled agility in David's soul on this and other worship occasions.

A theology of worship will reckon with the full spectrum of agility in the Spirit.

Agility in the Spirit encompasses grief. Twice in 2 Samuel,[18] grief precipitates David's worship. In other places, like Joshua, direct encounters with God precipitated worship. That connection is quite evident to us. It's not as obvious how grief precipitates worship. When his newborn son died, David went from confession to fasting, to grief, to worship.[19] The confession-and-worship connection is deep and widespread in the Old Testament. If confession and forgiveness (atonement) are ignored or compromised, worship is destroyed or seriously compromised. In addition to that connection, David, the man with such an amazingly agile spirit, also shows us the connection between grief and worship. David fasted in the hope of averting the disaster, but his infant son died. The grief David experienced was a different kind than it would have been if he had not fasted. Fasting didn't prevent the disaster, but it did change how he experienced it. Together, the fasting and the grief affected the worship that followed.

It's quite obvious how a direct encounter with however small a part of the glory and holiness of God would result in worship. It's less obvious to many people how a direct encounter with grief, an actual experience of it, would result in worship. But it does, when grief and worship become what grace and mercy make of them. How does grace-infused grief lead to, or prepare the way for, worship? It's not an academic, philosophical, or psychological question, though each of these may contribute to a response that, if adequate, will surpass them all. It is, ultimately, an inexplicable mystery how worship and its consequent joy are found in—or as a result of—grief. And it seems that the deeper the grief, and the more it is felt (not avoided), then the deeper the joy, and the more it is felt—not just said to be so. In the depths of grief, the depths of worship and joy merge. This is only so by the mercy and grace of God. It becomes another encounter, after all, with the glorious goodness and holiness of God. No wonder, then, that worship flows from the apparently unlikely experience of grief. ∫

[1] 2 Samuel 7

[2] 2 Samuel 6

[3] 2 Samuel 12:20 and 15:32

[4] 1 Samuel 13:14 and Acts 13:22

[5] Psalm 5:7, NIV

[6] Psalm 27:4, NIV

[7] Psalm 48:9, NIV

[8] Psalm 43:3-4, NIV

[9] Psalm 65:4, NIV

[10] Psalm 69:9, NIV

[11] Psalm 84:1-2, NIV

[12] 2 Samuel 6, NASB

[13] 2 Samuel 6:5

[14] 2 Samuel 6:10

[15] 2 Samuel 6:12

[16] 2 Samuel 6:14

[17] 2 Samuel 6:17

[18] 2 Samuel 12:20 and 15:32

[19] 2 Samuel 12:13-20

# 1 kings

Everything about the house of God was for this purpose: that God would dwell there. And He did. "The priests could not stand to minister because of the cloud: For the glory of the LORD had filled the house of the LORD."[1] This glory was real and the priests saw it. It was not just by faith that glory filled the house of God.

After Solomon's temple was built and dedicated,[2] God met with Solomon again as he had at Gibeon when He gave Solomon the wise and understanding heart Solomon had requested. In this meeting after the dedication of the temple, God assured Solomon of the best possible future for the house of God:

*The LORD said unto him, I have heard thy prayer and thy supplication, that thou hast made before me: I have hallowed this house, which thou hast built, to put my name there for ever; and mine eyes and mine heart shall be there perpetually.*[3]

God would actually live with them, in His house; his eyes and heart would be with them perpetually. As surely as people could find their way to the place where other people lived, so surely they could find their way to the place where God lived, the house of God. This building was not just filled with people, faith, prayer and the reading of Scripture. No. The house of God was most of all, and best of all, filled with the actual presence of God. The people came in order to approach and enter into what was already so, not just to ask for it. God's actual presence, His eyes and heart, made his house a home. We know a house doesn't matter much if it doesn't contain a home.

And we, even the most academic, professional, or scientific among us, know that home is a heart matter. Not a sentimental, squishy, lopsided matter—rather a real, full-heart matter.

The house of God is far more a heart matter than even our homes. Far more, in fact, because what happens there happens *in actual contact* with God. What happens at the house of God is about divine-human interaction. It's about the eyes and heart of God, present to receive us. It's about being seen, really seen and known, by God. It's about being taken into the center of God's being, into His heart. The problem is that it is beyond us to fully grasp or comprehend this. But it is real, and the power and love of it, the glory and holiness of it, forever surpass the very best of all human-to-human love we have ever known, or heard about, or dreamed of or wished or hoped for.

A theology of worship will show us a simple and certain path that leads to a hallowed house where the eyes and heart of God are there for us—perpetually. *k*

[1] 1 Kings 8:11
[2] 1 Kings 6 and 8
[3] 1 Kings 9:3

# 2 kings

David, God's man with God's heart, really wanted to build a house for God. But it was David's son Solomon who fulfilled this desire. The building and vessels and furnishings were all prepared with love and the greatest care and skill—for God. This was a place to receive God, and God did come and dwell there. God's glory filled the house. So much so that his priests could not endure it. All the people knew God was with them, not just by faith, but in glory right there in the temple.

By the end of 2 Kings this longed-for and much-loved house of God was burned, and the beautiful, enduring metalwork it contained was broken in pieces or carried off.

What an enormous, unthinkable loss. The book of 2 Kings ends so sadly. How could the old people in Judah, or even the young people, ever hope to know again the wonder and comfort of God's house filled with God's glory in their very midst? They were so broken and so scattered.

It's in the heart of God's people to want real worship. When God's house is taken from them, and the glory of God's presence is gone, how do they follow the longing of their hearts that still draws them to worship? What becomes of worship when the people of God are broken and scattered?

A theology of worship will be with the exiles suffering the unthinkable loss of God's glory among them, the unthinkable loss of God's house. A theology of worship will tune in to their pain; it will follow them into captivity; it will listen to and observe with ever-deepening respect how longing for worship revived the hearts of the exiles. It will recognize the sad parallels today as the hearts of the broken and scattered people of God try to find their way to restored worship.

Before the temple was destroyed and the people scattered into exile, there was terrible oscillation back and forth between good and evil in Israel and in Judah, and it was played out in the house of God. The way that Israel's and Judah's kings paid tribute to, or appeased, the rulers of other nations also affected the house of God. At times, hallowed things were taken from the temple and sent to the ruler of another nation.[1] Both the spiritual condition of Israel and the political interactions with other nations registered in visible, felt ways in the house of God. During a time when the nation and its beloved but also beleaguered temple were careening toward disaster, Josiah demonstrated fierce love and loyalty for worship. It's clear how *much* Josiah and others wanted to avoid what happens at the end of the book.

While the house of God was being repaired, the book of the law was found. When the scribe read it, King Josiah rent his clothes and sent the priest, the scribe and his servant to Huldah the prophetess. Josiah searched for God and God's will. He found out the wrath of God would not be changed,[2] but because Josiah's heart was tender, and he humbled himself before the LORD, and rent his clothes, and wept before the LORD,[3] God heard Josiah and would give him a peaceful death, sparing him from seeing the dreaded outcome.[4]

After Josiah received God's message from Huldah, he went into action with remarkable passion[5] that reveals far more than cerebral truth at the heart of worship. Josiah's passion also shows something very different from tolerance for, or acceptance and maintenance of, the status quo. It was *not okay* that the house of God contained altars to other gods, a grove, and other corruption. It was *not okay*. Josiah smashed the corruption to pieces, then ground it into a fine powder and cast the dust of the corruption onto the graves of the children of the people and into the Kidron brook. And he burned the grove. Eradicated it completely. Josiah wasn't being nice and conciliatory with the worship style that had developed in the temple, nor with the people responsible for it.

At the heart of worship there is a flammable passion. Josiah shows us:

> *And like unto him [Josiah] was there no king before him, that turned to the LORD with all his heart, and with all his soul, and with all his might, according to all the law of Moses; neither after him arose there any like him.*[6]

A theology of worship will show us the timeless truth. It will show us the full range of Josiah's passion. The man who smashed the corruption is the same man who, with tender and humble heart, had searched for and responded to God with tears. The passion that compelled Josiah was born of a tender and humble heart. It was a God-empowered, life-affirming passion. A theology of worship will show us the way of God-empowered, life-affirming passion, whether we are in a position with leadership influence or just one of God's people with a longing for restored worship. *k*

---

[1] 2 Kings 12:18
[2] 2 Kings 22:17
[3] 2 Kings 22:19
[4] 2 Kings 22:20
[5] 2 Kings 23:2,6,12,15
[6] 2 Kings 23:25

# 1 Chronicles

In the final chapter of 1 Chronicles, David spoke to the whole congregation for the last recorded time. He blessed the LORD before all the congregation, and then he said to all the congregation, now bless the LORD your God. And all the people of the congregation blessed the LORD God, and bowed down their heads, and worshipped the LORD. Then they made Solomon king, and David soon died in a good old age, full of days, riches, and honor.

As I consider what David might have said in his final message to the congregation, I imagine he might have focused on family, or on aspects of his fame as king. He had many children, and many conquests and victories. He could have blessed each child. He could have reviewed the most significant military conquests during his reign. He could have outlined what it would take for subsequent kings to make the most of what he had built for them.

The book of 1 Chronicles could have ended many ways. The way it does end doesn't mean David didn't bless each of his children. It doesn't mean he didn't review significant conquests or advise subsequent kings. But the ending of 1 Chronicles does show the top priority for this book, and for David's life. In his last message to the congregation David says, "Now I have prepared with all my might for the house of my God.... Moreover, because I have set my affection to the house of my God...."[1] Everything else in David's overflowing life—all his family, all his national loyalties—everything revolved around this. Building a house for God was the desire of David's heart. Everything else David was and did for the people had this at the center, making everything possible and giving it all purpose.

As pilgrims in the desert, they had pitched their tents around the sanctuary, around God's visible presence with them. Now as they settled in their homeland to stay, it wouldn't be right, they wouldn't really be fully at home, until they were gathered around the house of God again. This time it would be with God's house permanent—just like theirs were becoming. This is what the nation needed in order to really be who it was, and fully at home. David knew it. They were a people who had been given their history and their future by God's house in their midst. Whatever David had to say to or about his children, and whatever he had to say to or about the nation, it was secondary and served this ultimate desire of his heart: to build a house for God. His affection and all his might were given to this.

Although David did not get to build the temple, he did all he could for the sake of it. Most of all he brought the Ark to Jerusalem. After "the Ark had rest," David set Heman, Asaph, and Ethan (each a Levite) over the service of song in the house of the LORD.[2] When the Ark—the heart of God's dwelling with them—was set in the tent that David pitched for it, David "appointed certain of the Levites to minister before the Ark of the LORD, and to record, and to thank and praise the LORD God of Israel: Asaph the chief, and next to him Zechariah, Jeiel, and Shemiramoth, and Jehiel, and Mattithiah, and Eliab, and Benaiah, and Obed-edom: and Jeiel with psalteries and with harps; but Asaph made a sound with cymbals; Benaiah also and Jahaziel the priests with trumpets continually before the Ark of the covenant of God."[3] Then David delivered a psalm into the hand of Asaph and his brethren to thank the LORD.[4]

Somehow this picture, and what was happening in it, needs to settle into our souls. Asaph and his brethren, and beyond them all Israel whom they represented, were drawn to be as close as possible to the Ark. What they longed for the most was also the thing they feared and reverenced the most: the presence of God. At the Ark, God's holy, glorious presence was actual. How they responded to the Ark was a matter of life and death. Their longing, and holy fear, and actual closeness to God are what cause the psalms and the music to be what they are. When our hearts enter into that kind of longing, holy fear, and awareness of the actual closeness of God, then psalms and worship music are what they are meant to be. Longing, vibrant reverence, a keen sense of the holy, and closeness to God—these are the most foundational sounds of psalms and worship music. The rest is either built on this foundation, or else it isn't worship music.

How *does* a person realize, enter into, and expand the longing, reverence, and sense of the holy that are gifts of God in his or her soul? A theology of worship will respond to this question. Among other things, that response will show how personal and congregational worship combine with a life of daily communion with God. Congregational worship and personal communion with God influence and shape each other. *C*

[1] 1 Chronicles 29:2,3

[2] 1 Chronicles 6:31ff

[3] 1 Chronicles 16:4-6

[4] 1 Chronicles 16:7

# 2 Chronicles

*Then the priests brought the Ark of the covenant of the LORD to its place, into the inner sanctuary of the house, to the holy of holies, under the wings of the cherubim.[1]*

This happened after Solomon finished building the house of God that was filled with gold and garnished gems and beautified with images of cherubim.[2] It really must have been a wonder to see. Natural and glorious, everything about it served reverence. The Ark was the first and most essential item placed in this wonderful, prepared place. Placing the Ark was not done by movers or workmen. It was done by a large, very large, assembly of national leaders consisting of elders, heads of tribes, chiefs of the fathers of Israel, the king, and the Levites who actually carried the Ark.[3] And all the congregation of Israel assembled with King Solomon before the Ark, and they sacrificed sheep and oxen, so many they couldn't count them. It's difficult to take in the size and significance of the event, all that was involved in placing the Ark in the glorious new house of God.

Immediately after telling of unnumbered sacrifices, the account continues, "And the priests brought the Ark… to its place…."[4] Then the priests came out of the holy place, where at the east end of the altar there were singers in white linen, having cymbals and psalteries and harps. With these singers there were 120 priests sounding with trumpets.

*It came even to pass, as the trumpeters and singers were as one, to make one sound to be heard in praising and thanking the*

*LORD; and when they lifted up their voice with the trumpets,*
*and cymbals and instruments of musick, and praised the LORD,*
*saying, For he is good; for his mercy endureth for ever: that then*
*the house was filled with a cloud, even the house of the LORD; So*
*that the priests could not stand to minister by reason of the cloud:*
*for the glory of the LORD had filled the house of God.*[5]

One day in January, when we hadn't seen sunshine for a long
time, the clouds began to clear away. I was surprised how far south
the sunshine originated. I looked up; maybe I was making sure it was
the sun. Or maybe it was just to say, "What do you know, the sun
shone in this south window from over the corner of Amaya's house,
right up there." I'm not just sure why I looked. But in a flash I was
reminded *not to do that*. The glory and power of the sun overwhelmed
my eyes.

The glory of the LORD that filled the house of God was as
real and as visible as the sun that shone that day over the corner of
Amaya's house into our window. Only that glory wasn't the sun. It
was the presence of God. It was God accepting human hospitality.
God saying, "I will live in the house you built for me."

After the Ark was in place, King Solomon blessed the LORD.
To do this, he prayed before the altar on a brazen scaffold where he
knelt down before all the congregation of Israel, spread his hands
toward heaven, and said, "O LORD God of Israel, there is no God
like thee in the heaven, nor in the earth; which keepest covenant, and
shewest mercy unto thy servants, that walk before thee with all their
hearts." The prayer continues,[6] and it shows how central the house
of God was and would be. Everything about their life centered there.
Even if they were to sin, even if they were carried into captivity, their
life would still center there.[7]

When Solomon finished praying, "fire came down from heaven,
and consumed the burnt offering and the sacrifices; and the glory of
the LORD filled the house. And the priests could not enter into the
house of the LORD, because the glory of the LORD had filled the
LORD's house. And when all the children of Israel saw how the fire
came down and the glory of the LORD upon the house, they bowed
themselves with their faces to the ground upon the pavement, and

worshipped, and praised the LORD, saying, For he is good; for his mercy endureth forever."[8]

When have I (and the people I have gone to church with, anywhere), when have we bowed with our faces to the ground and worshipped—because fire came down from heaven and the visible, unbearably bright glory of God filled the place of worship? The book of 2 Chronicles (especially chapters five, six and seven) shows that worship flowed from, and involved, an actual encounter with the glory of God. Are our hearts meant to be satisfied with anything less? In my head I hear phrases such as, "The kind of glory that filled the temple changed. Now it's Jesus. Don't expect light and glory." My heart responds to such thinking by knowing that Jesus surpasses by *encompassing*, not excluding, glory. Jesus, the sandal-clad Carpenter, is also the LORD of the Old Testament. He was and will always be both. My face needs to go to the ground in confession asking that I might stop dividing our One God into two, the Old Testament God and the New Testament God. My face also goes to the ground in the hope of encountering the Holy One through Jesus Christ my Lord. I need a sandal-clad Carpenter who is compassionate enough to veil his glory; and I also need to encounter the glory and have worship ignited in my whole being. This kind of need is expressed in David's heart longing—a longing I share: I will not be satisfied until I find a place for the LORD, a dwelling for the Mighty One of Jacob.[9]

When Jesus fills the house, there is glory. To experience less than glory speaks of clouds, and buildings, and maybe even caves, but it does not dim the sun. To set my heart on finding a place—a dwelling—for Jesus the Mighty One of Jacob is to set my heart on a place where the glory of God breaks through.

After the Ark was placed and glory filled the house; and after Solomon prayed and fire fell from heaven and glory filled the house, then began days of feasting. When these were done, Solomon "sent the people away into their tents, glad and merry in heart for the goodness that the LORD had showed unto David, and to Solomon, and to Israel his people."[10] "Thus Solomon finished the house of the LORD."[11]

What a finish, what a dedication! How do we take it in? Years of longing, with David's heart (and the hearts of how many others of God's people!) set on this, went into this wonder-filled experience. David's longing to build a house for God—to offer hospitality to God—must have been contagious. The people around couldn't help but hear about the one thing that mattered most to him. Knowing a man with a heart like this changed the heart of others. The longing in David's heart became a great groundswell in Israel. When the Ark came to rest in the house of God, and the glory of God filled the house, then this groundswell of heart longing in Israel found soul-satisfying fulfillment. It was good. So very good. The joy of the Israelites was transposed to new heights and depths as they worshipped and prayed in song:

*For He is good;*
*For his mercy endureth for ever.[12]*

After the dedication services were complete, the LORD appeared to Solomon by night. Have you ever needed to reflect with a loved one about all that happened at a special occasion? What endearing compassion, that God would come to Solomon after this splendid occasion was over!

*Then the LORD appeared to Solomon at night, and said to him,*
*"I have heard your prayer, and have chosen this place for Myself*
*as a house of sacrifice.... My eyes shall be open and My ears*
*attentive to the prayer offered in this place. For now I have chosen*
*and consecrated this house that My name may be there forever,*
*and My eyes and My heart will be there perpetually."[13]*

"My heart will be there perpetually" expresses divine yearning, heart-longing, that is tender and strong beyond—far beyond—our comprehension. We can't dream or imagine enough to take it in. How do people respond to this vast divine heart that is perpetually present in His house? No answer to that question is ever enough, yet there are good beginnings. For example, they do it by entering into the longing in their own hearts. They do things that help them recognize and foster their longing to know the heart of God. Human heart longing is our heritage. It is the human counterpart to the heart longing of God. This human heart longing is our birthright as children of God. We respond to the vastly tender and strong heart of divine love by claiming our birthright with humble gratitude, gratitude that keeps growing forever.

The book of 2 Chronicles is one big, grand opening into worship. It offers a great deal to a theology of worship. *C*

---

[1] 2 Chronicles 5:7, NASB

[2] 2 Chronicles 3:6,7

[3] 2 Chronicles 5:4

[4] 2 Chronicles 5:7, NASB

[5] 2 Chronicles 5:13,14

[6] 2 Chronicles 6:14-42

[7] 2 Chronicles 6:36-38

[8] 2 Chronicles 7:1-3

[9] Psalm 132:3-5, NIV

[10] 2 Chronicles 7:10

[11] 2 Chronicles 7:11

[12] 2 Chronicles 5:13

[13] 2 Chronicles 7:12,15,16, NASB

# Ezra

Ezra records restoration. Jewish people who had been captives for many years returned home. Yet was it anything like home as they, or their parents, had known it? What did they see? Were they like slaves given freedom? Or prisoners now paroled? Perhaps they had no momentum. They simply weren't geared up for reconstruction, even though Cyrus, the one with power to hold or free them, had given them authority and resources for reconstruction. Ezra scholars describe them as "lethargic." Although they were rejoicing in freedom, they were apparently in a kind of stupor.

Seeing ruins that had to be dealt with before reconstruction could even begin would be daunting. They also saw, and heard about, the people of lands close by and were terrified of those people. There was much that was pitiful about their return.

In the midst of these pitiful conditions, worship begins to be restored. They had come home again, to a home that had to be rebuilt. And home for Israel always had the house of God in its center — worship at the heart. Gathered there, at the heart, in sacrifice and worship, they would maintain their identity and be revived.

The altar, with burnt offerings morning and evening, was the starting-place for reconstructing home and worship. This could be, and was, done quickly. The altar, and the morning and evening offerings, were a way to say, "Forgive me. Forgive us. And show us the way to Your heart again."

Ezra tells about this time, a time when hope, terror, joy and grief converged with deep intensity. When the foundation of God's house was laid, many who had seen Solomon's temple wept with a loud voice. At the same time many shouted aloud for joy. The people shouted with a loud shout, and the noise was heard far away. Those who heard the people's cries couldn't discern the shouts of joy from the weeping. Restoration of the place of worship elicited strong feelings that were openly expressed.[1]

Confession also elicited strong feelings. Ezra prayed and confessed, weeping and casting himself down before the house of God, and a very great congregation of Israel gathered to him, and the people wept bitterly. All the men of Benjamin and Judah trembled.[2] Through confession, they found their way to their hearts. Through their hearts, they found their way to confession. This was the path that would take them all the way home again into the heart of worship. A theology of worship will show the necessary, the absolutely essential, connection between heart-full confession and worship. Ezra's short and pathos-filled account opens us to recognize and explore the connections between worship and our deepest, most intense hope, fear, grief and joy. *e*

[1] Ezra 3:11-13, NASB
[2] Ezra 10:1,9, NASB

# Nehemiah

Nehemiah tells how the book of the Law of Moses was read to the congregation of Israel, and how they responded. Positioned on (not behind) an elevated pulpit prepared for this purpose, Ezra, the priest and scribe, began by opening the book. When the people saw him do that, they all stood up. Then Ezra blessed the LORD, the great God. And all the people answered Amen, Amen, and lifted up their hands. And they bowed their heads and worshipped the LORD with their faces to the ground.

Standing again, the people listened as several men read and explained the law, causing the listeners to understand. As they heard and understood the words of the law, the people wept. And they were comforted: "Don't mourn; don't weep. Don't be grieved, for the joy of the LORD is your strength."[1] Their bodies, and minds, and feelings—their whole beings—were very much involved.

In this chapter (eight) and the next chapter, Nehemiah opens into worship that is packed with meaning. A theology of worship will pursue what these chapters reveal about whole-person worship, about confession and worship, and about law and worship. For example, "all the people wept, when they heard the words of the law."[2] Law and tears combined makes the law a matter of the heart.

The people of the congregation may have wept because now they could receive the law even though they weren't priests. Before this time, the priests had been the custodians of the law. Now the congregation was also made custodian of God's words. This brought the congregation closer to God; it consoled the people, and they wept.

They may have wept because in hearing the law they realized how painful sin is, for them and for God. We may not be sure of exactly why they wept, but reflecting on possibilities such as these gives us appreciation for the fact that they did weep, and they were assured the joy of the LORD was their strength. Worship happened; hearts broke; joy strengthened. Worship includes this kind of heart-healing, soul-satisfying encounter with the law.

To hear the law with less than a broken heart and strengthened joy is to miss the point of the law. To worship without a heart-breaking, joy-strengthening encounter with the law is to miss the point of worship. To recognize how the law is positioned as the vital nucleus in the heart of the house of God is to forever defeat legalism and works. A theology of worship has much to show us about these matters of the heart.

Confession and continuing worship follow the chapter eight account of the reading of the law:

*And they stood up in their place, and read in the book of the law of the LORD their God one fourth part of the day; and another fourth part they confessed, and worshipped the LORD their God."*[3]

Their prayer of confession began this way:

*Blessed be your glorious name, and may it be exalted above all blessing and praise. You alone are the LORD. You made the heavens, even the highest heavens, and all their starry host, the earth and all that is on it, the seas and all that is in them. You give life to everything, and the multitudes of heaven worship you.*[4]

What a prayer! What a "find" Nehemiah 9 is! How it leads us in the way of confession and worship! We can ponder and thrive on its timeless truth over and over. It shows us the way of confession that is shaped by the Spirit of God and integrated with worship. Worship gives confession its context, its hope, its destiny. Confession gives worship its door. Confession and worship are life-giving companions. A theology of worship will show us the way of Spirit-shaped confession combined with worship. *N*

---

[1] Nehemiah 8

[2] Nehemiah 8:9

[3] Nehemiah 9:3

[4] Nehemiah 9:5,6, NIV

# Esther

The book of Esther speaks about worship the way it speaks about God—without words. Is there a moment in history when the Jewish people were any lower or any more threatened? During the time of the judges, and during the time of the kings, the people of God had oscillated between good and evil, between obedience and corruption, with consequent devastation. The low times of evil tragically compromised and weakened their life as a people. The most painful blows fell in the house of God, when holy vessels were carried off to (or by) another king or country. Painful blows fell when corruption moved into the house of God in the form of altars to other gods and when the services in God's house were replaced by a mingling of what God wanted and what God did not want.

When the too-frequent low points of evil in Israel were at their lowest, the enemy would strike at the heart of all by taking the Ark of the Covenant. Having the enemy do this—cut out the heart of the house of God—was to the soul of the Jewish people what the cruelest torture is to the body of a prisoner of war. The Jews had been to this deep level of devastation, and even then there had been hope of recovery.

But now, in the book of Esther, the Jews faced an end that would take them beyond the hope of recovery. This brought "great mourning among the Jews, and fasting, and weeping, and wailing; and many lay in sackcloth and ashes."[1] At the dedication of the house of God, when the glory of God had filled the house of God, Solomon prayed that God's people would find refuge and be rescued from various threats by going into God's house and praying. If, as a consequence of sin, they were carried away into captivity, then Solomon prayed they would return to God with all their heart and soul and pray toward their land, toward Jerusalem, and toward the house of God.[2]

Did the grieving Jews in Esther's time do that? Did they pray the way Solomon hoped captive Jews would pray? The book of Esther is silent about such specifics. With this silence Esther may be showing us the depths of their departure from the ways of worship and prayer that were their heritage, their birthright as Jews. But this silence, as well as the remarkable absence of any name for God in the book of Esther may, instead, be showing us the vast extent of God's compassion.

The book of Esther doesn't open into worship by saying, "Here's what worship is, and here is how it is done." But Esther does open into worship by showing how the infinitely compassionate God, who isn't even named in Esther, responds to the broken, grieving heart of His people who are humbly acknowledging their desperate need. That is how worship ignites in the heart of God's people. *e*

[1] Esther 4:3
[2] 2 Chronicles 6:38

# Job

There came a messenger and said to Job, "The Sabeans stole all the oxen and killed the servants."

Another messenger came, who said, "Fire from heaven burned up the sheep and the servants."

A third messenger came and said, "The Chaldeans stole the camels and killed the servants."

A fourth messenger came and said, "Your sons and daughters are dead."

Then—when hearing that his children were dead—"Job arose and tore his robe and shaved his head, and he fell to the ground and worshiped."[1]

When the house of God was being consecrated, the children of Israel saw fire come down from heaven and consume the burnt offering and the sacrifices. They also saw the glory of God upon the house of God. They responded by bowing with their faces to the ground and worshipping.[2] Worship followed an actual encounter with the fire and glory of God. Even when we haven't experienced the same kind of dramatic encounter with God, we can understand how worship would follow. They go together.

But do unthinkable amounts of suffering and grief go with worship? We are less ready to understand and accept this. Yet here, as with David,[3] deep grief combines with worship. This calls us to come to terms with the mystery of this unlikely union of grief and worship. Who would *worship* when experiencing unthinkable losses and grief? Job would. Job did. People like Job still do. A theology of worship will show us how. It will open us to begin to comprehend and experience that graced moment when unthinkable grief touches, and even merges with, the deepest and most divine joy. The suffering of God and the joy of God combine only because the mercy and power of God make this possible. We can't explain it, much less require it of another person. But we can enter this mystery and know the wonder of it happens. A theology of worship will ponder this mystery and draw us into it.

In addition to opening into the combination of grief and worship, Job is a corrective that keeps us from seeing humility and confession — a contrite heart — for what it isn't.

The books that precede the book of Job show that the altar is the way into worship. Sin is a mystery at work in the world. It is so blatant it's hardly believable; and so insidious it's hardly detectable. Sin isn't just out there in the world; it's in here in my life. *I* have sinned, and here is how. My heart, my tears, and this innocent lamb come to the altar to acknowledge the mystery of sin and to find the surpassing mystery of atonement. The altar was the place for seeing the most despicable, and the most deceptive, things for what they really are; and it was also the place for seeing and receiving the forgiveness and compassion of God for what *they* really are. This was the way into worship.

People are continually drawn into the blatant and insidious mystery of sin, making it necessary to continually return, with contrition, to the altar. *That is not all.* Job shows that a person is not just a sinner forever discovering new layers of contamination in his soul. Job is a perfect and upright man. God said so. Job knew it. He didn't back down; he didn't believe that his suffering was caused by his sin.

The Plan of God — salvation — has been compared to a golden thread that runs through all history. Everything else in the world's history relates to that thread. Within an individual's life, God's salvation is also a golden thread. Some people recognize and cherish the golden thread with all their heart. Job did. Nothing, not even the most cruel, intense suffering, caused him to let go of it. Job was an Old Testament incarnation of Romans 8:38, 39: "For I am persuaded that neither death, nor life, nor angels, nor principalities, nor powers, nor things present, nor things to come, nor height, nor depth, nor any other creature, shall be able to separate us from the love of God, which is in Christ Jesus our Lord."

A theology of worship will show us both the way of contrition and the way of confidence in the righteousness God gives. It will keep us aware of the crucial connection between this combination (contrition and confidence) and worship. ⫟

---

[1] Job 1:20, NASB
[2] 2 Chronicles 7:3
[3] 2 Samuel 12:20

# Psalms

The sung prayers of the people of God through the ages all open into worship. They do this in snatches (a few verses at a time); they do it in chapters (a complete psalm at a time); and they do it best in the entire book. Praying our way through the entire book of Psalms, over and over, is the best way to experience them as the opening into worship that they are. They speak from heart and to heart as they lead us into the heart of worship.

The book of Psalms is solidly historical and more. "There is little clear internal evidence by which to associate particular psalms with known historical events."[1] Grounded in history, the psalms are also timeless. Even during the centuries (maybe 900 years) when they were being composed and compiled, the psalms were not just about that time and place. They drew people beyond their time and place to other times and places on earth, and beyond earth to heaven. The place of worship the psalms refer to is sometimes in Jerusalem and sometimes in Heaven. At times it seems intentionally ambiguous. The sanctuary that is being referred to may be on earth or in heaven.

The psalms offer us life for both the heartwork that precedes worship and for the heart of worship. They "school" us in the longing and reverence that are everywhere through the psalms. They lead us from obligatory psalm praying into heart-full psalm praying. Here are some of the ways they contribute to a theology of worship:

⚜ The first and last psalms (Psalm Five and Psalm 138) that contain the word worship say, "I will worship toward thy holy temple." When in captivity, the people of God were to worship toward Jerusalem and the temple. When in God's house,[2] they still worshipped toward God's holy temple—in heaven. "Worship toward" involves a heart set on and inclined there; a heart entering into what happens there. A theology of worship will help us worship toward God's holy temple. It will show us the way into an earthly place of worship, and from there on into the heavenly place of worship.[3]

A theology of worship will show us how we can grow in the fear and reverence of God. Fear and reverence mean the same thing, yet we need both words (and more!) in order for the full significance of each to begin to unfold.

- "Unite my heart to fear thy name."[4] All aspects of our being converge in our heart. We need help with gathering, or uniting, all of these aspects together into the essential focus of fearing and reverencing God's name.

- "As the heaven is high above the earth, so great is his mercy toward them that fear him."[5] "As a father pitieth his children, so the LORD pitieth them that fear him." The flow of God's mercy and pity for us is connected with fear and reverence and the consequent worship. Each of these three (mercy, reverence and worship) contributes to the other two. We need help with entering into this more and more fully.

- Psalm 119 talks about God's servant who is devoted to God's fear (verse 38). The servant of God doesn't just fear or reverence God, but is also *devoted* to that fear and reverence. We need help with knowing—actually entering into—this degree and quality of fear and reverence.

- "There is forgiveness with thee, that thou mayest be feared." Relief comes with being forgiven. Most of us

know this by experience. Some of us also know that
intimacy and compassion come with the forgiveness of
God. But how many of us have actually entered into an
increase in fear and reverence as a part, or result,
of forgiveness? We need help with realizing—knowing
by experience—that forgiveness does increase fear and
reverence, and how it does this.

- "The LORD taketh pleasure in them that fear him, in
  those that hope in his mercy."[6] There's a connection
  between reverencing God and hoping in his mercy. We
  need help with realizing and living into this connection.

🎵 A theology of worship will lead us to love and reverence the
place of worship (and what happens there) in the timeless
ways the psalmist did. Temple, sanctuary, tabernacle, and
most of all house of God are terms used to describe God's
dwelling place among us—the place where the psalmist
wanted to dwell. The psalms show that dwelling in God's
house was life-giving and deeply satisfying; it was *the one
thing* the Psalmist desired and sought after.[7] The Psalm (23)
that has become most universally known and cherished
culminates with this desire, this best possible outcome:
"I will dwell in the house of the LORD forever."[8]

Dwelling in the house of the LORD is about a place to
which we go—God's house (sanctuary, church, place of
worship). It's a real, tangible, physical location like the
rooms we live in. In addition, dwelling in the house of the
LORD is about being, even while still on earth, a part of
the heavenly sanctuary.

To "dwell" in God's house includes being at home.
Dwelling in the house of God we are at home in a holy
place, with The Holy One, the One we fear and reverence
with all our heart. Like the psalmist, we would rather be at
home in this holy place with this Holy One than anywhere

else, with anyone else. Like the Psalmist, we will love to be in the physical location where this "dwelling with" is most tangible and most realized. In this physical, here-and-now house of God, the larger reality of participating in the heavenly sanctuary is also known heart-to-heart as vividly and as surely as we know we are in the house of God and not in our own house.

The psalms are prayers to be sung with ever-deepening awareness of their meaning and how they serve communion with, and reverence for, God. A theology of worship will lead us in this kind and quality of communion with God. 𝒫

---

[1] *Seventh-day Adventist Bible Dictionary,* p. 911. Reprinted with permission from the *Seventh-day Adventist Bible Dictionary,* copyright by Review and Herald Publishing Association. This book may be purchased online at www.adventistbookcenter.com.

[2] Psalm 5:7

[3] See also Psalms 63:2; 68:24; 73:17; 77:13; 96:6; 150:1

[4] Psalm 86:11

[5] Psalm 103:11,13

[6] Psalm 147:11

[7] Psalm 27:4

[8] See also Psalms 5:7; 43:3; 46:4; 48:9; 52:8; 61:4; 65:4; 84:1, 4,10; 92:13; 132:2-7

# Proverbs

"Be thou in the fear of the LORD all the day long."[1] The book of
Proverbs doesn't contain the word worship; nor does it contain the
words altar, house of God, sanctuary, temple, or tabernacle. Proverbs isn't trying to tell us what worship is and where and how to do
it. Yet Proverbs contains this opening into worship: "Be thou in the
fear of the LORD all the day long." And repeatedly Proverbs makes
the point that everything that matters most (wisdom and understanding) begins with the fear of the LORD.[2] We can't even get to what
the book of Proverbs is about if we don't fear the LORD. And when
we do fear and reverence the LORD, how can we avoid worship?
Maybe we can, but we certainly can't worship without fearing and
reverencing the LORD. So Proverbs, by emphasizing the fear of the
LORD as it does, is an opening into worship. How well it does this
for us has much to do with how willing and able we are to do more
than make an assumed backdrop out of the fear of the LORD. In
other words, it isn't enough to say, "Of course I fear God; that's a
given."

Because I have never walked into a room for an in-person, face-
to-face appointment with God, I'm afraid my fear of God is more
theoretical than actual. As I realize the too-often theoretical nature of
my fear of God, humility (companion to the fear of God[3]) comes to
my rescue; it gives me a clearer view of how limited I am in actually
fearing and reverencing God. This same rescuing humility gives me
prayers like these: Show me the kind of fear of You, God, that is a
fountain of life. Help me know in my heart — my whole being — that

all the wisdom and understanding I might ever have, or hope for, flow from fearing and reverencing You, God. Humility frees me from assumptions that would continue to distance me from the actual fear and reverence that are the fountain of wisdom, understanding and all the rest of life.

With humility comes comfort in the awareness that it is possible to be in the fear of the LORD all the day long. Fearing and reverencing God don't just happen at special locations at special times; the fear and reverence of God is for every day. Worship that needs to happen and does happen in congregations at special times also happens in individual hearts, every day. That's comforting.

The heartwork that prepares the way for worship, and the heartwork that worship is, are both encountered in various places in Proverbs.[4] Its emphasis on the heart is another way Proverbs opens into worship, even though it's a book that is sometimes seen as secular, or ethical, and not very religious. $\mathcal{P}$

---

[1] Proverbs 23:17

[2] See Proverbs 1:7; 9:10; 14:26,27

[3] See Proverbs 22:4

[4] For examples see Proverbs 4:23; 15:30; 16:1; 18:12; 23:7; 27:19

# Ecclesiastes

*Keep thy foot when thou goest to the house of God, and be more
ready to hear, than to give the sacrifice of fools: for they consider
not that they do evil. Be not rash with thy mouth, and let not
thine heart be hasty to utter any thing before God: for God is in
heaven, and thou upon earth: therefore let thy words be few.[1]*

This is a rather unexpected opening into worship that may at first
seem incidental or marginal in Ecclesiastes. Watch your step as you
go to church. Maybe that involves being aware and watchful about
just where you are going and why. Maybe it involves a caution that
a person can fall or get off the track even on the way to worship. So
watch your step—go, humbly aware that you need caution and protection. There's more in this and the next verse. In the house of God,
be ready to hear, don't be rash with your mouth or hasty in your
heart. Instead, maintain this humble perspective: God is in heaven,
and you are on earth. Seeking to receive and maintain awareness
of heaven—to really be with this reality—this is enough to keep us
humbly aware that we are earthbound still. Earthbound but connected with God who is in heaven. That's not incidental or marginal
at all.

There is another opening into worship in Ecclesiastes. This one
is *over all* and *in all*. It is the conclusion of the whole matter: "Fear
God and keep his commandments."[2] Worship always includes fear
of and reverence for God. And experiencing and expressing fear and
reverence are acts of worship. Can we have one (fear or worship)

without the other? It's hard to see how we could, not when each of them is being what it is meant to be. Each makes the other necessary. The path to fear and worship in Ecclesiastes is privileged, tragic, sad, and ultimately triumphant. It takes Solomon and all similar seekers through extremes. The most desirable things—character traits like wisdom, material prosperity, power, accomplishments, success and influence—are abundant. Yet the privileged one is reduced to a deep sense of futility. The heights of privilege, power, and personal appeal all collapse. Nothing is left but meaninglessness. Nothing... except for repentance. In humility and repentance the privileged-now-disillusioned one finds his way into fear and worship that conclude the whole matter—triumphantly. Ecclesiastes sets worship in the context of life, privileged life, with all of its hopes, ideals, and disillusions. A theology of worship needs the chapter Ecclesiastes gives it. This is especially so in privileged cultures where plenty (economically, technologically, scientifically, and in many other ways) gives way to futility and disillusions.

---

[1] Ecclesiastes 5:1,2
[2] Ecclesiastes 12:13

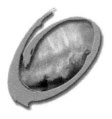

# Song of Songs

There is something my heart knows, something it has tasted and wants more and more of. I'm not alone in this heart-knowing and this desire. What my heart knows and desires more all the time is this: Worship happens when we realize that the Love of Our Life is divine. In worship we actually encounter The Holy One—and know always-greater depths of reverence and love. All forms of human love show us the way to this Ultimate Love, which infinitely outshines them all. The Song of Solomon is willing to risk words about it. Without even knowing for sure, at each point in the book, who is talking to whom, a Spirit-guided person can be drawn into love, and from there on into Love, by this song.

Without being inappropriately scholastic or sentimental (and without trying to resist or defend allegory), a theology of worship will show us that this sumptuous, prodigal book opens into the Love of Our Life—the Divine, Holy Love of our Life. ʃ

# Isaiah

Isaiah saw the Lord sitting upon a throne, high and lifted up, and His train filled the temple. Above the throne were seraphim that each had six wings: with two he covered his face, with two he covered his feet, and with two he flew. "And one cried unto another, and said, Holy, holy, holy, is the LORD of hosts: the whole earth is full of his glory."[1]

This experience of God conditioned everything Isaiah did, said, and was as the prince of prophets in Israel. His immediate response was, "Woe is me! for I am undone; because I am a man of unclean lips, and I dwell in the midst of a people of unclean lips: for mine eyes have seen the King, the LORD of hosts."[2]

When Isaiah responded like that, one of the seraphim laid a coal from the altar on his mouth and his iniquity was taken away and his sin purged. Then he heard God say, "Whom shall I send, and who will go for us?" Isaiah replied, "Here am I; send me."[3] Then God said to tell the people that although they were hearing and seeing, they were not understanding or perceiving.

This encounter with the glory of God, and the worship that surrounds God, humbled Isaiah into confession, forgiveness, and from there into being the prince of prophets.

This experience wasn't just there and gone, like a passing dream. It followed and sustained Isaiah. It remained with him as a shaping influence — through everything. It was an opening into worship that stayed open, showing Isaiah the way. It kept surrounding and sustaining him. It faithfully cautioned and comforted him. Isaiah kept seeing and perceiving the glory of God and the worship He receives from seraphim and deserves from us. This experience flavored and empowered everything he did, said, and was. As we understand and perceive this, it will shape and influence our worship.

Isaiah has been described as a gifted orator and poet whose unsurpassed beauty of style and expression made his book into the literary masterpiece of all Hebrew literature. It's also been said he used a richer vocabulary than that found in any other Old Testament book; a glossary of Isaiah would list more than 2,000 individual words. This gifted man of words—words that were all affected by that living coal from the altar—shows us at the end of his book that everything culminates in worship:

> *And it shall come to pass, that from one new moon to another,*
> *and from one sabbath to another, shall all flesh come to worship*
> *before me, saith the LORD.*[4]

There is a groundswell of worship throughout the Old Testament. By the end of Isaiah this groundswell takes each person and all nations into its power. Isaiah is the one most gifted at showing us how the Messiah—the Jehovah of the Old Testament and the Jesus of the New Testament—is the power in this groundswell. Because of Isaiah, and those who echo his message, if not his style, the people of God (the ones who do understand and perceive) are prepared to receive Jesus of Nazareth as the culminating power in this groundswell, the One who sums and surpasses all.

A theology of worship will help us explore Isaiah's vast openings into worship. It will prepare us to receive and worship the One who sums and surpasses all. It will show us the vastness of what He encompasses, and how we can respect and know the vastness and give God the worship He deserves. It will show us how we can first recognize, and then survive, the weight of glory in Jesus Christ our Lord. A theology of worship will spare us from reducing Jesus to less than He is.

Isaiah's openings into worship are constant companions[5] and ultimate culminations,[6] each affecting everything else in Isaiah. A theology of worship will walk us into these vast openings and cause us to be increasingly reverent and at home there. [6]

[1] Isaiah 6:3

[2] Isaiah 6:5

[3] Isaiah 6:8

[4] Isaiah 66:23

[5] Isaiah 6

[6] Isaiah 66

# Jeremiah

The word worship is used only twice in Jeremiah.[1] Both times, Jeremiah is instructed to stand in the gate, or the court, of the LORD's house and proclaim God's word to those who come to worship the LORD. "Speak all the words that I command thee to speak unto them; diminish not a word." The chapter seven context shows the extremes of spiritual deterioration, which included polluting God's house by setting their abominations there. They trusted in lying words and didn't realize how their hearts were both deceived and deceptive. Blind, deceived and determined, they kept saying, "the temple of the LORD, the temple of the LORD, the temple of the LORD." God sent Jeremiah to the house of God, where deception and deterioration were the worst, to confront the people and be willing to tell them what they didn't want to hear. The people may have been going to the right place, and on the right day, but true worship wasn't happening: not at all. If they didn't reckon with conditions at the house of God, the complete desolation they were headed for would happen. Obedience (faithfulness to the covenant, including keeping the ten commandments) and worship were meant to be life-giving, deeply joyful complements, each serving and beautifying the other. But that life-giving combination of obedience and worship wasn't happening.

Their precarious position at the brink of utter desolation was a matter of the heart—a deceived heart. Several times Jeremiah told the people so.[2] Without omitting the hard part, Jeremiah summed up God's message to the people: "The heart is deceitful above all things, and desperately wicked: who can know it?"

The life-giving combination of obedience and worship that would spare them from desolation was also a matter of the heart—a God-knowing, God-fearing heart. Several times Jeremiah told them so.[3] He said that they needed to search for God with their whole heart, and know and fear God, Who would put His law in their inward parts, and write it in their hearts.

Their false worship was a matter of a deceived heart; the true worship they desperately needed was also a heart matter—a matter for a God-fearing heart. A theology of worship will not omit the hard words about this matter of the heart! Just how does a person, and how does a church, seek God with its whole heart? A theology of worship will show us how, because it is a matter of life and death; true worship won't happen without seeking God and knowing Him with a whole heart. How does a person, how does a church, recognize it has received a heart to know God? How does a person, how does a church, know God's law is written in its heart? A theology of worship will deal with questions like these. It will spare us from giving the head, or any other aspect of our being, inappropriate preeminence. It will increase our awareness of the multifaceted splendor of the heart, and how it is that every aspect of our gloriously complex being converges there, and how—in this center of our whole being—we meet with and respond to the Spirit of God. A theology of worship will not fail us in this matter of the heart.

Jeremiah provides another opening into worship that's especially difficult to enter in a way that begins to be adequate:

*My tabernacle is spoiled, and all my cords are broken: my children are gone forth of me, and they are not: there is none to stretch forth my tent any more, and to set up my curtains.[4]*

*I have forsaken mine house, I have left mine heritage; I have given the dearly beloved of my soul into the hand of her enemies.[5]*

These verses show an impossibly sad reversal of the day when the glory of God filled the house of God.[6] In doing that, they invite us into the heart of God. Deep reverence and tender, strong compassion prepare us to be guests there. As receptive guests in the heart of God, we may begin to know what it was like for God to be at home — in His house — with Israel. We may begin to sense the yearning in God's heart when he said, "Let them make me a sanctuary that I may dwell among them."[7] We may experience reverent wonder at the awareness that God wanted something so much, something that only His children could give.

As reverent, compassionate guests in the heart of God, could we come to a better awareness of what makes the house of God so important to God? Could we know more fully what he wants to have happen there? Could we begin to know His joy in being with us, and His grief when there is no one to stretch forth his tent any more?

A theology of worship will help us be reverent, compassionate guests in the heart of God, who really hear and respond to God's heart about the place of worship and its services. ⌐

[1] Jeremiah 7:2 and 26:2

[2] Jeremiah 9:8; 17:9; 23:26; 42:20; 49:16

[3] Jeremiah 24:7; 29:13; 30:21; 31:33; 32:39, 40

[4] Jeremiah 10:20

[5] Jeremiah 12:7

[6] 2 Chronicles 5:13,14 and 7:1-3 tell about that glad day.

[7] Exodus 25:8

# Lamentations

"My sighs are many, and my heart is faint."[1] This book of laments and prayers expresses massive grief. The pain of Judah's desolation and the destruction of the temple is intensified by guilt. "See, O LORD, for I am in distress; my spirit is greatly troubled; my heart is overturned within me, for I have been very rebellious."[2] "The joy of our heart is ceased; our dance is turned into mourning. The crown is fallen from our head: Woe unto us, that we have sinned! For this our heart is faint; for these things our eyes are dim."[3] The heartwork of Lamentations is so much more than intellectual grappling with a problem or an intellectual exercise. Lamentations in its way, just like the rest of the Bible in its way, reveals full-fledged heartwork. Heartwork opens into worship. In the case of Lamentations, it is an extremely sad route to worship, but a sure route.[4]

The New American Standard Bible titles the final chapter of Lamentations "Prayer for Mercy." The prayer doesn't include the word mercy, but it's clearly a cry for mercy with a poignant ending:

> *Thou, O LORD, dost rule forever;*
> *Thy throne is from generation to generation.*
> *Why dost Thou forget us forever;*
> *Why dost Thou forsake us so long?*
> *Restore us to Thee, O LORD, that we may be restored;*
> *Renew our days as of old,*
> *Unless Thou hast utterly rejected us,*
> *And art exceedingly angry with us.*[5]

Worship infuses the very cry for mercy with life and hope. The cry for mercy is expressed to the One whose throne is from generation to generation—the One the praying person worships. Worship makes the cry for mercy so different from what it would be without worship. Worship conditions and shapes the cry for mercy. It also becomes the culmination. Recipients of God's mercy worship the Giver. That God can and will have mercy and forgive inspires awe and produces worship. A theology of worship will sensitize us to this and show us how to live its truth more and more fully. ⌐

[1] Lamentations 1:22

[2] Lamentations 1:20, NASB

[3] Lamentations 5:15-17

[4] The Bible shows this in various ways, one is in Psalm 130:4

[5] Lamentations 5:19-22

# Ezekiel

*As the appearance of the bow that is in the cloud in the day of rain, so was the appearance of the brightness round about. This was the appearance of the likeness of the glory of the LORD. And when I saw it, I fell upon my face, and I heard a voice of one that spake.[1]*

This mysterious vision of God can be approached again by those whose hearts are set on worship. It can groom our sense of the grandeur and glory of God. Today's seekers can also claim the best that previous seekers have found in this vision, setting aside whatever trivialization or explanation that may get in their way. This vision is a vast opening into worship that may be there most of all so we can fall on our faces like Ezekiel, and go into our work with worship as our frame of reference. A theology of worship will help us do so.

The book of Ezekiel begins with worship as the prophet's frame of reference; and at its end, Ezekiel culminates in restored worship. At the beginning of his difficult work, Ezekiel fell on his face when he saw the glory of the LORD.[2] This worship affected and supported everything Ezekiel was and did. The end of his book comes around to the beginning—worship. "The glory of the LORD filled the house of the LORD; and I fell upon my face."[3] I recognize like never before how worship "hems in" everything else in Ezekiel. I can't hope to adequately perceive and receive the rest of the book if I don't see it all through the eyes of a worshipper who is moving toward a culmination that is also worship. Worship is at the center of everything, giving heart and strength. I need to realize this in order to understand Ezekiel; and I need to realize this in order to understand the unfolding of events for God's people today.

As the book of Ezekiel moves from worship to worship, it opens into various aspects of worship. One of those is how Israel related to holiness. The people of Israel were God's people, yet tragically they polluted, defiled and profaned God's holy name — the name God had pity (or concern) for; he was jealous for it.[4] They also despised holy things,[5] profaned God's sabbaths,[6] and failed to differentiate between the holy and profane.[7] As part of their restoration, they would learn, or relearn, the difference between the holy and the profane.[8] By means of a theology of worship, we will learn, or relearn, the timeless truth about this difference, and how a worshipper will recognize and revere the holy.

Another of Ezekiel's openings into worship is so sadly presented in these words of God:

*How weak is thine heart.*[9]

*Can thine heart endure?*[10]

Israel was like a wife who commits adultery by taking strangers instead of her husband. This faithless infidelity to God demonstrated Israel's weak, even failing, heart. This condition came to utterly tragic extremes. Finally God said he would deal with it. Before he did, this spurned Lover who would not stop loving asked, "Can thine heart endure?" The whole excruciatingly painful experience is a matter of the heart. Israel's weak and failing heart is also likened to a heart of stone. God responded to their desperate condition by scattering them among the heathen to consume their filthiness.[11] But that's not all; He promised them a new heart. "A new heart also will I give you, and a new spirit will I put within you: and I will take away the stony heart out of your flesh, and I will give you an heart of flesh."[12]

Worship is what happens when we realize our Lover is divine, the Holy One. The tragic extremes portrayed in Ezekiel open into this perspective on worship. The Divine Lover takes drastic action, including the ultimate extremes of discipline, and also promises to give the people a new heart that is soft, strong and ready to receive Him, the Holy One, who is prepared to dwell with them again. It couldn't come out anywhere but worship when the glory of the LORD fills the house of the LORD again.[13] Although the outcome of that prophecy was different from what had been first anticipated,[14] worship remains the culmination, and it takes a soft, strong heart to get there. A theology of worship will show us this way of the heart. It will prepare us to recognize when our heart is weak. It will ask us, "Can your heart endure?" It will relay God's promise of a new heart of flesh, and show us how to receive it. A theology of worship will take us by way of the heart into worship where we will know our Lover is divine, the Holy One.

There is another way that Ezekiel opens into worship. This way involves special comfort and hope. Ezekiel, a priest and prophet, was exiled with a group of Jews at Tel-abib, by the river Chebar. They may have lived a reasonably normal life, at least socially and economically. But they were far from their heart. They were far from the sanctuary, the center of their worship, which was the desire of every faithful Jew. What Ezekiel prophesied about the sanctuary must have deeply distressed them: "Thus saith the Lord GOD; Behold, I will profane my sanctuary, the excellency of your strength, the desire of your eyes, and that which your soul pitieth."[15] Ezekiel and the cluster of Jews where he lived maintained a life that looked normal, yet was very far from being what faithful Jews longed for. Normalcy of a sort may have alleviated some of their suffering; but it more likely intensified the loss and distress they felt about the sanctuary and its services. Circumstances, if not their neighbors, seemed to be saying, "Never mind that everything that matters most to you is far away, inaccessible to you, and that it will be destroyed, and you will never see it again. Never mind, just settle into normalcy." But this didn't work for faithful Jews who loved God's house and all that it included. They suffered keenly. God knew they would, and here's His special comfort for them: "Thus saith the Lord God: Although I have cast them far off among the heathen, and although I have scattered them among the countries, yet will I be to them as a little sanctuary in the countries where they shall come."[16] When the house of God, and all it includes, is not accessible to us, where do we go? What becomes of our God-given desire for His house? Can we hope that the center of our life as a people, and the center of our individual response to God will survive? Can we worship when our place of worship is gone? Will normalcy, with all its conveniences and demands, destroy our desire for worship? Ezekiel offers comforting and hope-filled responses to questions like these. Ezekiel opens into some of the most personalized and compassionate dimensions of a theology of worship. *E*

[1] Ezekiel 1:28

[2] Ezekiel 1:28

[3] Ezekiel 44:4

[4] Ezekiel 36:21; 39:25; 43:8

[5] Ezekiel 22:8

[6] Ezekiel 22:8,26

[7] Ezekiel 22:26

[8] Ezekiel 44:23

[9] Ezekiel 16:30

[10] Ezekiel 22:14

[11] Ezekiel 22:15

[12] Ezekiel 36:26, see also Ezekiel 11:19; 18:31

[13] Ezekiel 44:4, see also Ezekiel 43:4,5.

[14] For one commentary on the restoration portrayed in Ezekiel 34-48, see the *Seventh-day Adventist Bible Dictionary* regarding the Book of Ezekiel.

[15] Ezekiel 24:21

[16] Ezekiel 11:16

# Daniel

*Thou, O king, hast made a decree, that every man that shall hear the sound of the cornet, flute, harp, sackbut, psaltery, and dulcimer, and all kinds of musick, shall fall down and worship the golden image.*[1]

The sound of it out there on the open plain of Dura must have been dramatic, and perhaps magnificently beautiful. "The sound of the cornet, flute, harp, sackbut, psaltery, and dulcimer, and all kinds of musick" is repeated four times in ten verses in Daniel 3. Through repetition of this cumbersome, yet almost musical phrase, the chapter reinforces its point, beyond avoidance. Fall down and worship. When you hear the sound of the cornet, flute, harp, sackbut, psaltery, and dulcimer, and all kinds of musick, worship—like Nebuchadnezzar told you to worship. Do it or die.

All the people did as they were told, except Shadrach, Meshach and Abednego. These three would not worship the golden image. They would rather die than worship any god, except their own God.[2]

Daniel definitely opens into worship, here and in other powerful ways. So much converged and climaxed on the plain of Dura. There was the will of a monarch intent on establishing a kingdom that would last forever. The will of three men who didn't see it the monarch's way. And the will of God who gave them all life and choice. Everything that made the king who he was, everything that made the three dissidents who they were—the loves, joys, fears and hopes of their whole being—converged there. And everything that makes the

Holy One the only One worthy of worship. Everything about the life of these humans and this God climaxed in the issue of worship.

When my whole being (with all its loves, joys, fears and hopes) and worship come together, what happens? How do my being and worship touch and shape each other? I can ponder that to good advantage. In this and other ways, a theology of worship can help me and others follow the Daniel 3 opening into worship.

Later in his book (in the third of four parallel lines of prophecy),[3] Daniel tells of a vision where a saint said to him, "Unto two thousand and three hundred days; then shall the sanctuary be cleansed." What if we could, without any damage to prior truth about this text, also see how it opens into worship? Cleansing restores the sanctuary to its full purpose, the always-best part of this purpose being that the sanctuary is the place where God dwells. Cleansing makes it the place, again, where the glory and holiness of God are known and actually and reverently approached. Cleansing gives luster to glory again, or perhaps it only removes the blurring smudges from our lenses. Cleansing of the sanctuary also means that through contrition, confession and forgiveness, the people approach and respond to that now-splendid-again glory.

Imagine how that kind of cleansing reverberates in worship; how it restores worship to its intended fullness. Maybe we have more to claim in the promise of the cleansing at the end of the 2300 days. A theology of worship can help us find out.

This vision that promised sanctuary cleansing included deeply disturbing aspects. It was so troubling that Daniel fainted and became sick. The vision astonished him, but he didn't understand it. Some time later, while still seeking an understanding of it, Daniel said, "I set my face unto the Lord God, to seek by prayer and supplications, with fasting, and sackcloth, and ashes: And I prayed unto the LORD my God, and made my confession...."[4] While Daniel was still expressing contrition and confessing his sins and the sins of his people, Gabriel came to give him understanding because Daniel was loved so much.[5] The compassion of God merged with, and far surpassed, Daniel's contrition and confession. In that blessedness, understanding unfolded. Gabriel told about the finish of transgression, an end of sins, reconciliation for iniquity, and the coming of everlasting righteousness. He explained that these things, and the confirmation of the covenant, would come with the Messiah the Prince, who would be cut off. In Gabriel's visit, Daniel was tasting the very mercy—the divine saving power—that would come in unthinkable ways in the future. Daniel was given understanding that would serve his continuing comprehension of the incomprehensible. That comprehension continues in the lives of the people of God who are still astonished (now in retrospect) at the events the vision portrayed. What an opening into worship!

In the second of the four parallel visions, Daniel saw the throne of the Ancient of Days. It was a throne like fiery flame where thousands upon thousands, ten thousand times ten thousand, stood before him and ministered to him. Then Daniel saw one like the Son of Man come with the clouds of heaven to the Ancient of Days where he was given dominion, and glory, and a kingdom, that all people, nations, and languages, should serve him; his dominion is an everlasting dominion, which shall not pass away, and his kingdom that which shall not be destroyed. This is one of the most crucial and most majestic of all the Old Testament openings into worship. There are, of course, so many openings into worship, and they all overflow with wonder. Individually and together they are so important to us. Then, it is as if this crucial Daniel seven opening gathers them all together. This magnificent opening into worship deserves our repeated exploration and utmost respect and reverence. A theology of worship will show us how to live into the wonder and majesty of this opening. We need hearts that are soft and strong and expanded beyond our imagination in order to ever survive in such majestic country, and worship appropriately there. 𝌆

---

[1] Daniel 3:10

[2] Daniel 3:12,18,28

[3] The *Seventh-day Adventist Bible Dictionary* article about the book of Daniel shows the parallels in the four lines of prophecy (Daniel 2; Daniel 7; Daniel 8-9 and Daniel 10-12).

[4] Daniel 9:3-4

[5] Daniel 9:23

# Hosea

Hosea shows us God loving Israel as a faithful, infinitely loving and long-suffering husband. This infinite, divine love is lavished on a people whose heart is taken away by whoredom.[1] Ephraim made many altars to sin.[2] Hosea's account of the size and perseverance of God's faithfulness and the size and perversity of Israel's faithlessness opens into worship in two ways, one so positive, the other so tragic. Hosea, like the Song of Solomon, shows God as the Divine Lover of His people. A theology of worship will help us receive this picture into our hearts where we can ponder and respond to it with the kind of love it deserves. Worship happens when we realize our Lover is divine. In worship, all the best we know of human love, certainly marital love, is escalated into a holy encounter that can't be reduced to words. But a theology of worship will help us find our way beyond words and into this opening.

The other opening Hosea offers is through the tragedy of spiritual adultery. Ephraim made many altars to sin. The altar was a place of worship. How does such spiritual, worship adultery happen? What are the subtle first stages of it? How is it manifest? How does worship shift from true to false? What is it that makes spiritual adultery so treacherous and tragic?

A theology of worship will caution us with reflections on such questions. It will show us how spiritual adultery compromises, robs, and eventually destroys worship. It won't leave us caught in the tragedy of spiritual adultery, it will always return us to this hope: "For the ways of the LORD are right, and the just shall walk in them."[3] H

[1] Hosea 4:11    [2] Hosea 8:11    [3] Hosea 14:9

# Joel

What a picture Joel gives! His openings into worship are better realized with some of this picture planted in our heart. Here the already-condensed content of Joel is abbreviated even more.

Awake! Lament! The meat offering and the drink offering are cut off from the house of the LORD; the priests, the LORD's ministers, mourn. The harvest of the field is perished; the vine is dried up. "How do the beasts groan! The herds of cattle are perplexed, because they have no pasture; the flocks of sheep are made desolate." "The beasts of the field cry also unto thee: for the rivers of waters are dried up, and the fire devoured the pastures of the wilderness."[1]

Sanctify a fast, call a solemn assembly, gather into the house of the LORD your God, and cry unto the LORD. Blow the trumpet in Zion, sound an alarm in my holy mountain, tremble, for the day of the LORD cometh. Blow the trumpet in Zion, sanctify a fast, call a solemn assembly: Gather the people, sanctify the congregation. Let the ministers of the LORD weep between the porch and the altar, and let them say, "Spare thy people, O LORD, and give not thine heritage to reproach," why should the heathen rule over them and say, "Where is their God?"[2]

The Lord will answer and do great things. Be not afraid, ye beasts; be glad ye children of Zion; rejoice in the LORD your God: for he hath given you the former rain moderately, and he will cause to come down for you the rain, the former rain, and the latter rain. "Ye shall eat in plenty, and be satisfied, and praise the name of the LORD your God, that hath dealt wondrously with you." "And ye shall know that I am in the midst of Israel, and that I am the LORD your God."[3]

"The LORD also shall roar out of Zion, and utter his voice from Jerusalem; and the heavens and the earth shall shake: but the LORD will be the hope of his people, and the strength of the children of Israel. So shall ye know that I am the LORD your God dwelling in Zion, my holy mountain: then shall Jerusalem be holy." There will be new wine from the mountains; milk from the hills, waters from the rivers of Judah, and a fountain shall come forth from the house of the LORD.[4]

The last phrase in Joel's sweeping, dynamic and very condensed portrayal is this: "For the LORD dwelleth in Zion."[5]

The house of God is the place to gather in the face of tragedy. The holiness, the glory of God, and past worship experiences give the atmosphere that's needed. They give proportion and hope in the midst of dire, death-dealing circumstances. The bigger and more devastating the problem, the more urgent it is to immerse it in holiness, glory, and worship in the house of God. A theology of worship will help us do this. It will show us the way into holiness, glory and worship that is as real and vivid to us as the death-dealing circumstances of our individual and corporate lives. A theology of worship will not leave us without a strong sense of the holy; it won't offer us insipid or reckless worship; it won't stop until we reverently and actually know the glory of God as surely as we know death-dealing circumstances. Why should the heathen, or anyone, say Where is their God? "I *am in the midst of* Israel." "I *am* the LORD your God *dwelling in* Zion, my holy mountain." "*The Lord dwelleth in* Zion."[6] This is the great central and ultimate reality in Joel; it is the sum and conclusion of Joel. A theology of worship will show us how to receive and live it as our great central and ultimate reality also. ⨍

[1] Joel 1:8-20
[2] Joel 1:14-2:17
[3] Joel 2:19-27
[4] Joel 3:16-18
[5] Joel 3:21
[6] Italics added.

# Amos

"Go you seer, flee away!"[1] Amaziah, the priest of Bethel, didn't want Amos to prophesy any more at Bethel "for it is the king's chapel."[2] Worship was the way the priest and king of the northern kingdom of Israel wanted it. Go to Judah; prophesy there. Get out of here. Leave us alone to worship the way we've been worshipping.

Amos stayed and gave them the word of the LORD anyway. The sad chorus of his appeal to Israel was, "'Yet you have not returned to me,' declares the LORD."[3] Five times Amos repeated it. They observed feast days, gathered for solemn assemblies, and offered burnt offerings, meat offerings, and peace offerings, with the noise of songs.[4] "But ye have borne the tabernacle of your Moloch and Chiun your images, the star of your god, which ye made to yourselves."[5] Their worship was corrupt, and their morality mirrored this corrupt worship. They turned "judgment into gall, and the fruit of righteousness into hemlock."[6]

"Take away from Me the noise of your songs."[7] Those who have tried to patiently endure church music that isn't at all worshipful to them—these people can empathize with God's reaction to the noise of Israel's songs. That Amos should say something so contemporary could even bring a smile, if it were not so sad. The matter of worship music has, in fact, become such a consuming issue that it hardly seems possible to get past it for the sake of worship. This may be the saddest part of all about music at church. In other words, music, however important, isn't all that worship is about. Trying to satisfy very divergent music tastes is not the same as having a theology of worship. We could, miraculously, figure out how to satisfy the music taste of every person who comes to church and still be far from the heart, understanding and spirit of an adequate theology of worship.

But if we *could* take away not only the noise of church songs, but also the noise of words attacking and defending those songs, long enough to develop a theology of worship, it might set in motion a kind of miracle. Among other things, this would surely help us seek the LORD more than we seek songs about the LORD. Amos was contemporary about that also: "For thus saith the LORD unto the house of Israel, Seek ye me, and ye shall live: But seek not Bethel." Bethel was the center of worship in the northern kingdom, the place where not only the noise of their songs, but their other observances were corrupt. It was the place where the priest and the king were trying hard to preserve the status quo.

A theology of worship will help us go to the heart of this mat-ter—each individual and each local church beginning with its own heart—without making a whip out of the words of Amos. A

---

[1] Amos 7:12, NASB

[2] Amos 7:13

[3] Amos 4:6-11, NASB

[4] Amos 5:21-23

[5] Amos 5:26

[6] Amos 6:12

[7] Amos 5:23, NASB

# Obadiah

The brief book of Obadiah shows a relationship between two brothers and their families that went bad. Tragically bad. Broken and captives in Babylon, the descendants of Jacob wept when they remembered Zion. Their tormentors demanded songs of joy, saying, "Sing us one of the songs of Zion!" They couldn't imagine doing that. Instead their psalm continued this way:

> *If I forget you, O Jerusalem,*
>   *may my right hand forget its skill.*
> *May my tongue cling to the roof of my mouth*
>   *if I do not remember you,*
> *if I do not consider Jerusalem my highest joy.*
>
> *Remember, O LORD, what the Edomites did*
>   *on the day Jerusalem fell.*
> *"Tear it down," they cried,*
>   *"tear it down to its foundations!"[1]*

As Babylon destroyed Jacob's highest joy, Esau's descendants cheered them on. The Edomites were glad about what happened here:

> *Your foes roared in the place where you met with us;*
>   *they set up their standards as signs.*
> *They behaved like men wielding axes*
>   *to cut through a thicket of trees.*

*They smashed all the carved paneling*
*with their axes and hatchets.*
*They burned your sanctuary to the ground;*
*they defiled the dwelling place of your Name.*
*They said in their hearts, "We will crush them completely!"*
*They burned every place where God was worshiped in the land.*[2]

Revenge. Retribution. Vindication. Words like this describe what Jacob's descendants must have wanted very badly. But Obadiah—the prophet who wasn't letting the unthinkable behavior of the Edomites pass unnoticed—gave them this:

*...and there shall be holiness...*[3]

Holiness. Holiness opens into worship. Obadiah promised Israel holiness. Are we, and were they, accustomed to connecting devastated relationships, such as the one between Jacob and Esau, with holiness and its consequent worship? What good does it do to think or talk holiness and worship when the Edomites did what they did and it hasn't been set right yet? I fear that we don't make a practical connection between worship-producing holiness and the hard relational realities of life. But we really need to. A theology of worship will help us do it. It will help us claim the hope and healing that is meant to be ours when, in response to relational tragedies, we receive God's holiness and respond with appropriate worship. The more vivid the holiness and the more real and heartfelt the worship, the more the cry for revenge and vindication subsides, until it fades away entirely. ✺

---

[1] Psalm 137:5-7, NIV
[2] Psalm 74:4-8, NIV
[3] Obadiah vs. 17

# Jonah

*Out of the belly of hell cried I.... I am cast out of thy sight; yet I will look again toward thy holy temple.*[1]

When the temple was dedicated, Solomon asked God to hear the prayers of His people in a variety of circumstances.[2] In each circumstance, Solomon saw them praying in the temple or, if they weren't able to get to the temple, then toward the temple. One of the circumstances Solomon described was captivity. If while in captivity "they pray toward the house which I have built for thy name," Solomon prayed, "Then hear...and maintain their cause."[3]

Did anyone ever feel any more captive, and removed from the sight of God, than did Jonah inside the big fish? Captive in the belly of hell, Jonah did just what Solomon prayed he would; and God responded just as Solomon prayed He would. Jonah looked toward God's holy temple. He said, "My prayer came in unto thee, into thine holy temple."[4] He could have just prayed where he was, trusting God to meet him there in the dark. Most of us are pretty glad to know there isn't anything too small for God to notice or too big for God to do something about. And we're glad we can pray anywhere. I'm sure Jonah was too! But Jonah did more than rely on God to meet with him in the dark. In his prayer Jonah went to where God was—to God's holy temple. Doing this made his prayer worshipful, and it set his dire circumstance in the context of worship.

What have I learned about worshipful private prayer like Jonah's? What would God like to show me? What is worshipful prayer like — or what *could* it be like? A theology of worship will help us with questions like these. ⚜

---

1 Jonah 2:2,4

2 2 Chronicles 6:12-42

3 2 Chronicles 6:38,39

4 Jonah 2:7

# Micah

*Wherewith shall I come before the LORD, and bow myself before the high God? Shall I come before him with burnt offerings, with calves of a year old?*

*Will the LORD be pleased with thousands of rams, or with ten thousands of rivers of oil? Shall I give my firstborn for my transgression, the fruit of my body for the sin of my soul?*

*He hath shewed thee, O man, what is good; and what doth the LORD require of thee, but to do justly, and to love mercy, and to walk humbly with thy God?[1]*

When I bow before the high God, what do I bring? Burnt offerings? Year-old calves? Thousands of rams? Ten thousands of rivers of oil? My firstborn? The possibilities escalate to unthinkable extremes. The reply is calm and subduing: Do justly, love mercy, walk humbly with thy God. Bowing before the high God isn't what you're making of it. In fact, it's much more challenging than that, as any judge, teacher, parent or anyone else who has ever tried to administer justice knows. Any who have applied themselves to knowing and loving mercy also recognize the enormity of this simple requirement. And what proud heart, now learning humility, hasn't begun to recognize the stubborn tenacity of pride.

Bow before the high God as a just, mercy-loving, humble person. That's what God wants of worshippers. A theology of worship will help us see that *this* is not as easy as it would be to bring the most extravagant and unthinkable offerings. A theology of worship will help us see justice and the love of mercy, and humility, for what they are. It will also show us how our best attempts at justice, love of mercy and humility increase the meaning and acceptability of our worship. It will also show us how beholding God who delights in mercy[2] changes us, slowly but surely, into His likeness. What we bring (our humble attempts at being just, loving mercy and being humble) changes our worship; in turn worship (beholding our God who delights in mercy) changes us so that next time we bring more justice, more love of mercy and more humility to worship. A theology of worship will show us how to live into this dynamic exchange, more and more, for life. ⚔

[1] Micah 6:6-8
[2] Micah 7:18

# Nahum

When you think of Old Testament Assyria, what do you think of? My answer would be cruelty: powerful, extreme, terrifying cruelty. More than a hundred years before Nahum's prophecy, this same people had repented.[1] They had once repented and received God's forgiveness and escaped destruction, and by Nahum's time were at the crest of their national power; and yet, according to Nahum, they were doomed. Formerly repentant, now formidably powerful, and doomed. Turbulent extremes characterized this nation and those it touched and terrified. Nahum, who must have been a man of most remarkable courage and faith, took on their cruelty with poetry,[2] poetry portraying the vengeance and fury of God:

> *The LORD is slow to anger, and great in power,*
>   *and will not at all acquit the wicked:*
> *The LORD hath his way in the whirlwind and in the storm,*
>   *and the clouds are the dust of his feet.*
> *He rebuketh the sea, and maketh it dry,*
>   *and drieth up all the rivers:*
> *Bashan languisheth, and Carmel,*
>   *and the flower of Lebanon languisheth.*
> *The mountains quake at him, and the hills melt,*
>   *and the earth is burned at his presence,*
> *yea, the world,*
>   *and all that dwell therein.*
> *Who can stand before his indignation?*

*and who can abide in the fierceness of his anger?*
*His fury is poured out like fire,*
*and the rocks are thrown down by him.*[3]

It's just not possible to take it in. Calvary-sized Love is in con-
flict with the once-repentant cruel people. God wanted with all His
Divine Might to reach them through Israel, but how can that happen with Israel cowering under their cruelty? It is much too much to
take in, yet what comes through is this: God is God of ALL, including cruel terrifying Assyria and all the forces of nature. God is God
of ALL; he never was only Israel's God: never was, never would be,
never was meant to be. God is God of ALL. How does this settle
into our being when we worship? What differences does it make? A
theology of worship will help us know it, and take it in with all our
heart. N

---

[1] Jonah 3:5-10

[2] "The prophecy of Nahum is written in poetic style, its 1st chapter being an alphabetic
psalm...." *Seventh-day Adventist Bible Dictionary* p. 775. Reprinted with permission from the
*Seventh-day Adventist Bible Dictionary,* copyright by Review and Herald Publishing Association. This book may be purchased online at www.adventistbookcenter.com.

[3] Nahum 1:3-6

# Habakkuk

How can it, how *could* it ever be that way? Not when God is just and right. The book of Habakkuk expresses what hearts for centuries before and after him have suffered. When on a personal or public scale conditions first become unbearable, and then get worse, God's people hurt, struggle — and then insist that God respond to their agony. "I will stand upon my watch, and set me upon the tower, and will watch to see what he will say unto me, and what I shall answer when I am reproved."[1]

"And the LORD answered me."[2] The answer began with a call to faith and continued through a series of woes. Then — would we ever have guessed it? — the answer concludes with this:

"But the LORD is in his holy temple: let all the earth keep silence before him."[3] It is wonderful to be reassured of the justice and goodness of God when things are worse than we could have imagined they would get. But that is not all that Habakkuk, and we, receive. There is even more, and it is about worship. It's a surprise ending to God's answer. It is such a big surprise that many people neglect or overlook it to this day. How could the LORD being in his holy temple — the place of worship — help? What does that answer? How does that relate to the struggles-beyond-belief in our individual or corporate lives? It does. It does! And so wonderfully. A theology of worship will help us not overlook this. It will help us gladly receive the full response to Habakkuk, the one that is worship. It will help us see how worship calms us, how it reinforces our faith, clears our vision, and satisfies our hearts — how worship is the ultimate and very best answer we could hope for when things have gotten unbelievably difficult.

In his psalm-prayer of response, Habakkuk shows God coming, with His glory covering the heavens and the earth, then Habakkuk says,

*He stood, and measured the earth: he beheld, and drove asunder the nations; and the everlasting mountains were scattered, the perpetual hills did bow: his ways are everlasting.*[4]

What a picture—even the perpetual hills bowed in worship. Isn't it good! *H*

---

[1] Habakkuk 2:1
[2] Habakkuk 2:2
[3] Habakkuk 2:20
[4] Habakkuk 3:6

# Zephaniah

**G**od will famish all the gods of the earth, and everyone—all the coastlands of the nations—will bow down and worship God.[1] In these words Zephaniah promises two things: (1) the end of false worship when the gods of the earth have nothing left to sustain their existence, and (2) true worship of the true God by surrounding nations, not just Israel. A person could say Zephaniah, although apparently of royal descent, is about the "least" of the minor prophets—least known, least visible, least captivating, least memorable. Yet consider Zephaniah's grand view of the ultimate outcome in the ultimate issue of worship!

False worship degraded Israel; true worship would revive Israel and the surrounding nations. Worship makes, or, in the case of false worship, breaks a nation or an individual. True worship is a matter of the heart, encompassing the whole person. In worship we touch God's singular superiority, His holy compassion, and His law. In worship our hearts revive as we touch the divine by faith, and—in graced moments—in fact. True worship of the true God *makes* an individual, a church, a nation and the whole earth full of people. A theology of worship will help us see this, really see this, and take in its consequences, consequences that begin here and now and expand daily and weekly forever.

Zephaniah said something else about worship that is memorable, even if his style isn't. He said, "Her prophets are light and treacherous persons: her priests have polluted the sanctuary."[2] The history of Israel and Judah shows that subtle and blatant sanctuary pollution was associated with light and treacherous prophets. Did Zephaniah mean the kind of lightness that defines expected social and work-place interactions today? The don't-take-anything-too-seriously-laugh-instead kind of lightness that tries (sometimes successfully) to alleviate the suffering of our times? Perhaps Zephaniah didn't mean that kind of lightness; but then again, perhaps he did. However it was that light and treacherous prophets went with sanctuary pollu-tion in Zephaniah's day, there is likely to be a corollary today. Light and treacherous leaders are likely to still be associated with worship pollution. A theology of worship will show us the way to recognize and resolve this, no matter how subtle or difficult it is to see and do anything about. ✍

[1] Zephaniah 2:11 (See KJV, NASB and NRSV)
[2] Zephaniah 3:4

# Haggai

*"The latter glory of this house will be greater than the former,"
says the LORD of hosts, "and in this place I shall give peace,"
declares the LORD of hosts.[1]*

In this and the preceding verses, Haggai merges the past and
future of God's dwelling place on earth, and the worship that happens there. He begins by asking who was left that saw this house in
her first glory. The first temple had been destroyed sixty-six years
before. But in Haggai's day there were some who had seen, and
experienced, its glory. The materials and craftsmanship, and the
heavenly pattern for the building and its contents, created a structure
that was extraordinarily grand, beautiful, and best of all, worshipful.
Yet all of the temple's physical, material appeal was nothing when
compared to the glory of God that filled the temple. At the dedication
of the temple, this glory was so palpable — so brilliant and powerful — that the priests could not remain in the temple because of it.[2]

What was it like for those who did know the glory of the first
temple to be there in Haggai's day facing the ruins of the temple, and
the great difficulties of trying to rebuild? What a sad contrast they
were experiencing. Yet what an amazing thing Haggai was saying!
If they could hear, really hear, Haggai as well as they saw the former
glory and the present dejection; if they could anticipate as well as
recall, then they would survive. In fact they would be the first to do
what all of God's people since have been called to do: Let the glory of
the past serve the surpassing glory of the future.

By knowing and loving the former glory of God's house, they were prepared to receive and love the surpassing glory more fully. It wasn't just that Haggai wanted them to see how sadly different things were that made him ask who saw the house in her first glory. There were more important reasons for them to know the former glory. The more they had seen, touched and tasted the former glory (or been vividly told about it until they did see and taste for themselves), the more prepared they were to receive the surpassing glory that was coming. The glory of God accumulates, the later glory surpassing rather than eradicating the former. Who is there that saw the first glory? You are the ones most prepared to recognize and respond to the coming glory that will surpass that. Amazing. Head-shaking amazing to think that a surpassing glory was coming! A theology of worship will teach *us* to taste and see accumulating glory as fully as God intends us to know it. It will spare us from trying to delete the glory that has in fact been encompassed and surpassed. It will prepare us to receive the sandal-clad Galilean in the glory of His Incarnation, Death, Resurrection and Second Coming, and to respond with worship. *H*

[1] Haggai 2:9, NASB

[2] 2 Chronicles 5:14 and 7:2

# Zechariah

Jerusalem—the place where the temple was. The temple—the place where the Ark was. The Ark—the place where the most vivid presence of God was. The presence of God: this is what the people of God longed for; this is what they reverenced; this caused worship.

*If I forget you, O Jerusalem,*
  *may my right hand forget its skill.*
*May my tongue cling to the roof of my mouth*
  *if I do not remember you,*
*if I do not consider Jerusalem*
  *my highest joy.*[1]

How they loved Jerusalem! All their longing, all their reverence,[2] everything their heart was meant to be or express, all found their home, their ultimate expression and comfort, their satisfaction and fulfillment in Jerusalem—in worship. Jerusalem, as the loyal people of God knew it, was their highest joy.

Zechariah is a prophet of Jerusalem: he wants to know and he wants to tell what is going to happen at Jerusalem, the highest joy of God's people. All the families of the earth are to come to Jerusalem to worship:[3]

*The LORD shall be king over all the earth: in that day shall*
*there be one LORD, and his name one.*
*And it shall come to pass, that every one that is left of all the*
*nations which came against Jerusalem shall even go up from*
*year to year to worship the King, the LORD of hosts.*[4]

The other 11 of the minor prophets mention Jerusalem 24 times; Zechariah refers to Jerusalem 39 times. He says much about their highest joy. In doing that, Zechariah prepares us for the magnitude of the events in Jerusalem that were still in the future when he wrote, and the magnitude of events in the New Jerusalem that are still in the future as we read what Zechariah wrote.

A theology of worship will help the people of God today to know with whole and revived hearts what God intends us to know about Jerusalem and worship. Without becoming hopelessly sidetracked in sorting out which Israel and which Jerusalem a particular verse is referring to, our hearts can resonate with God's people of all ages past, present, and future for whom Jerusalem (as God intended it then and always) is their highest joy. Z

---

[1] Psalm 137:5,6, NIV

[2] Their reverence is usually referred to as fear of God, a reverent fear that was vital and life-giving to the people of God individually and corporately.

[3] Zechariah 14:17

[4] Zechariah 14:9,16

# Malachi

Malachi opens into worship through God's dialog with worship leaders who claim innocence; yet who are so guilty that God even cursed their blessings.[1]

The book of Malachi comes right after the book of Zechariah ends on a high note, anticipating a time when not only Israel but other nations would also go to Jerusalem to worship. Yet when Malachi wrote, about 100 years after Zechariah, worship at Jerusalem was so far from what God wanted that He said to the priests, "I have no pleasure in you…, neither will I accept an offering at your hand."[2] You offer polluted bread and say, "Wherein have we polluted thee?"[3] You have wearied the LORD with your words. Yet you say, "Wherein have we wearied him?"[4] Over and over the priests acted ignorant, and claimed to be innocent of wrongdoing. They kept asking "Wherein…?"[5]

For their own sake, and the sake of their congregation, the priests needed to honor,[6] fear[7] and glorify[8] God. Instead they were questioning whoever questioned them, even—or maybe especially—when the questioner was God. Trying to break through to them, Malachi said, "'If you do not listen, and if you do not take it to heart to give honor (glory) to My name,' says the LORD of hosts, 'then I will send the curse upon you, and I will curse your blessings; and indeed, I have cursed them already, because you are not taking it to heart.'"[9]

Listen to God and take it to heart. These two things could change everything—certainly worship—for the priests and their people. A theology of worship will show us the kind and quality of listening to

God that enable us to participate in worship. A theology of worship will also show us how to do the heartwork that is prelude and post-lude to worship and most of all the very pulse of worship itself.

*Listen to God and take it to heart.* O Malachi, as you end the Old Testament, how perfectly you prepare us for the next word from God—in the flesh. *M*

---

[1] Malachi 2:2
[2] Malachi 1:10
[3] Malachi 1:7
[4] Malachi 2:17
[5] Malachi 1:2,6,7; 2:17; 3:7,8
[6] Malachi 1:6
[7] Malachi 3:5
[8] Malachi 2:2
[9] Malachi 2:2, NASB

# Matthew

*Where is he that is born King of the Jews? For we have seen his
star in the east, and are come to worship him.
And when they were come into the house, they saw the young child
with Mary his mother, and fell down, and worshipped him.[1]*

What a way for Matthew to pick up where Malachi left off!
Malachi urged God's people to listen to God, and take to heart what
God says. Now the Word from God is a Newborn Infant—Who is
being worshipped.

But few did as Malachi urged. The Infant would grow into a
Man and say, "I speak to them in parables; because while seeing they
do not see, and while hearing they do not hear, nor do they understand. In their case the prophecy of Isaiah is being fulfilled, which
says,

*'You will keep on hearing,
    But will not understand;
And you will keep on seeing,
    But will not perceive;
For the heart of this people
    Has become dull,
And with their ears they scarcely hear,
    And they have closed their eyes
Lest they should see with their eyes,
    And hear with their ears,*

*And understand with their heart and return,*
*And I should heal them.'"* [2]

They didn't listen well and take to heart what God said in the
Newborn Infant who was worshipped. But we do. Look at all our
nativity scenes at Christmas. We get it. Too bad they didn't.

Is this really the case? When I try, at least to some small degree,
to imagine what it was like for the children of God with their Old
Testament heritage to listen and take this Infant Word from God
to heart, I'm cautioned. Cautioned because I begin to see parallels
between their struggle and mine. How could they ever combine
this surprising—stunningly surprising—earthiness and humanity
of Bethlehem with the divinity they worshipped when God's glory
filled the temple? They knew, for example, that you could not touch
the Holy Ark and live; yet here was a Holy Infant to be tenderly
cuddled? They couldn't unite divinity and humanity that way. As the
people of God, they would remain loyal to divinity.

Now, in our generation, the people of God know to be loyal to
the Newborn Infant. But carefully consider how many of us do it.
Many do it by denying the Old Testament heritage of worship. We
keep seeing and saying "Jesus *instead* of." "When Jesus came, that
was done away with" is so assumed and ingrained for many of us that
we rarely consider whether there is anything we might not be seeing or hearing that we still need to see, hear and take to heart. As the
New Testament people of God, we remain loyal to His humanity. In
other words, we are also guilty of not uniting divinity and humanity.

There is a way to enter humbly and courageously into the Incarnation—accepting both His divinity and His humanity. This humility
and courage will honor already-realized truth about how the Old and
New Testaments combine in their witness to worship. This humility
and courage will *also* enable us to hear, see and take to heart—more
fully than we have yet—how the Old and New Testaments combine
to show us what worship is, and how the people of God in all time
and eternity worship. ▲

---

[1] Matthew 2:2,11
[2] Matthew 13:13-15, NASB

# Mark

In worship we encounter, or prepare to encounter, the glorious presence of God. Alone as well as in a congregation, each of us can groom our longing for encounter with God's presence and glory. Each of us can foster an always-more-vibrant sense of the holy, and an ever-deepening reverence. There is always more that each of us can do on our way to encounter with the glorious presence of God. But the encounter is pure gift. Alone or congregated, we can't discipline our way into encounter with God's glory, and we can't produce the glory no matter how low or high the lighting or the decibels. Silence, sound, and setting may express our longing; they may support our sense of the holy and foster our reverence. But the glorious presence of God is a gift.

God gave this gift to Peter, James and John one day in a mountain setting. Mark's account of what Peter told about this encounter is utterly simple:

> *Jesus took with Him Peter and James and John, and brought them up to a high mountain by themselves. And He was transfigured before them; and His garments became radiant and exceedingly white, as no launderer on earth can whiten them. And Elijah appeared to them along with Moses; and they were talking with Jesus.*[1]

Whatever we think or make of Peter's suggestion to make three tabernacles, it is very clear that the disciples were frightened. Not just frightened, they were exceedingly afraid—terrified.

Some of us seem more susceptible to fear than do others. But there is a threshold when even fearless-seeming folks become fearful. Earthquakes are an example; as the Richter scale readings increase, there are fewer and fewer fearless folks. So with the glory of God. The more dazzling and present God's glory, the fewer fearless folks there are. Saying it isn't really fear doesn't change the fact that the fear of God is fear. However, and this makes a huge difference, for the people of God the fear of God is a holy fear. It attracts us with a most remarkable power. The fear of God is the raw form of reverence: it is its foundation. The fear of God gives life. It can't really be explained, but a theology of worship will help us enter into the fear of God. It will show us that holy fear frees us from destructive, faithless fear.

[1] Mark 9:2-4, NASB

# Luke

Fear and the holy entwine together in the first chapter of Luke more than in any other chapter in this Gospel. Zacharias was fearful, and the angel reassured him, saying "Fear not." The angel reassured Mary, saying, "Fear not." Mary magnified the Lord, saying, "His mercy is on them that fear him from generation to generation." John would be filled with the Holy Spirit from his mother's womb. Elisabeth was filled with the Holy Spirit. Zecharias was filled with the Holy Spirit. The ultimate life-giving and fear-inspiring indwelling of the Holy Spirit ever experienced by a human is included in this same chapter that is so full of fear and the holy. The angel told Mary that the Holy Spirit would come upon her, and the power of the Highest would overshadow her, and the Holy One born of her would be called the Son of God.[1]

Fear and the holy go together, and with them comes a mercy so tender and powerful that we can only begin to imagine or appreciate it. Although we never will fully comprehend God's magnificent mercy, holy fear will bring us closer and closer to it.

Holy fear happens when the Holy One touches our lives, and we notice. The more undeniable that touch, and the more wide-awake our response, the more holy fear and compassionate reassurance we will experience. If I claim the compassionate reassurance ("Fear not") *before* I even experience holy fear, what have I done? How have I intercepted the experience God wants me to have? Sadly, my calm assurance may mean I'm not very close to the Holy, or not noticing. If I minimize holy fear, even saying it is unnecessary, what have I done to my capacity for worship? A theology of worship will help us ponder these things in our heart.

Luke, like each of the Gospels, is a series of openings into worship. Everything in the Gospels prepares the way for the Cross and Resurrection. That doesn't mean each Gospel writer had in mind that each parable, miracle, teaching, or other event he wrote about would show us what worship is and how to worship. Rather, it means that everything that was happening, events rich in meaning, included a cumulative preparation for the Cross and Resurrection, with the consequent worship. A theology of worship will help us see this. It will help us do the heartwork that such awareness calls for. It will teach us how to ponder these things in our heart.

Luke ends — sums up his whole Gospel — with the praise and worship that follow the Cross and Resurrection.

> *And he led them out as far as to Bethany, and he lifted up*
> *his hands, and blessed them.*
> *And it came to pass, while he blessed them, he was parted from*
> *them, and carried up into heaven.*
> *And they worshipped him, and returned to Jerusalem with*
> *great joy:*
> *And were continually in the temple, praising and blessing God.*
> *Amen.[2]*

---

[1] See all of Luke 1
[2] Luke 24:50-53

# John

Jesus said, "No one can come to Me, unless the Father who sent Me draws him…. It is written in the prophets, 'AND THEY SHALL ALL BE TAUGHT OF GOD.'"[1] What a lifeline these words provide! They are jewels set in the midst of a chapter that is central to worship. These words assure, comfort and steady our hearts that might otherwise faint at the various ways this chapter is studied, taught, argued and defended. We need a way to be with Jesus, as He is given to us through the words of John 6. We need a way that is direct and life-giving, to let these words settle into our soul ever more completely. Jesus assures us of that way: The Father draws. We will all be taught of God.

With that enormously compassionate reassurance, we can press on to receive this chapter that opens so magnificently and so unthinkably into worship. It comes to this:

*Those who eat my flesh and drink my blood abide in me, and I in them.*[2]

As the Father revealed to Peter, He also reveals to us: Jesus is the Holy One of God.[3] It takes a very soft and a very strong heart to stay with the Jesus of John 6. Among other things, staying with the Jesus of John 6 has earth-shaking consequences for worship. The more we assimilate John 6, the more profoundly it affects our experience of worship.

Exodus gives us wonderful background for receiving the Jesus of John 6. The house of God, the dwelling place of God on earth and all the glory and worship associated with it, was established with this reason for its existence at its heart: "Let them make me a sanctuary, that I may dwell among them."[4]

When John introduced Jesus, he said, "The Word was made flesh, and dwelt among us."[5] The will of God, the desire of God's heart, is to dwell among us. He did it in the Old Testament sanctuary and temple, and He did it in Jesus of Nazareth.

It is more, even, than Jesus dwelling among the people of Palestine. When we stay with the Jesus of John 6, we go from the glory of God dwelling in sanctuary and temple, to the glory of God dwelling in the person of Jesus among the people of Palestine. Incredibly, but it *must* be believed and lived, we go on from there to this same Jesus dwelling in each person who eats his flesh and drinks his blood. It takes a very soft and a very strong heart to truly stay with the Jesus of John 6.

Some people choose the Old Testament grandeur and reverence instead. They don't accept the Jesus of John 6. He isn't divine enough for them.

Other people choose Jesus of Nazareth, saying they believe in his divinity, but they don't experience the holy fear of, the reverence for God and worship that happens when actually in the presence of the holy. These people rely on His humanity, and only have a belief about his divinity.

In order to stay with the Jesus of John 6, it takes a keen and reverent sense of the holy combined with a genuinely humble appreciation of Jesus' humanity. The grandeur and glory of God combine with the compassionate humanity of God's Son. If we had been there at the dedication of Solomon's temple, we would be more prepared to realize what a stretch it is for any human being to receive this divine-human union. Here's what they experienced:

> *It came even to pass, as the trumpeters and singers were as one,*
> *to make one sound to be heard in praising and thanking the*
> *LORD; and when they lifted up their voice with the trumpets and*
> *cymbals and instruments of musick, and praised the LORD,*
> *saying, For he is good; for his mercy endureth for ever: that then*
> *the house was filled with a cloud, even the house of the LORD; So*

*that the priests could not stand to minister by reason of the cloud: for the glory of the LORD had filled the house of God.[6]*

That glory was not done away with. That glory is encompassed and surpassed in Jesus of Nazareth. To receive Him is to touch the Holy, not just to handle the human. It takes a very soft and a very strong heart to stay with the Jesus of John 6. A theology of worship will help us do it. It will show us the worship that reverberates in the soul of a person who does stay with the Jesus of John 6. J

[1] John 6:44,45, NASB
[2] John 6:56, NRSV
[3] John 6:69, NASB
[4] Exodus 25:8
[5] John 1:14
[6] 2 Chronicles 5:13,14

# Acts

The magnitude of worship is very great. It is an immense topic. How does a person, or a church, develop a theology worthy of the topic, a theology both grand and simple enough? The book of Acts is a good place to look for help with that question. Jesus Christ, His life, death and resurrection, is the immense topic dealt with in Acts. Peter, Stephen and Paul each lead the way in making Jesus known. Luke's account of what they said and did reveals how very encompassing they were, and how very essential. Encompassing, because of the sweep of what was included in both the person and the presentation of each, of Peter, of Stephen and of Paul. Essential, because they knew what needed to be said and done, and they stayed with it, with a grand and effective simplicity. Nothing stopped them, not arguments, not threats, not intimidation, not complications or the immensity of their topic. Any of these might prevent a theology of worship from being developed, but none has to. Not when there are people of God like Peter, Stephen and Paul to show us the way and give us hope.

It's important to notice what they encompassed: the will of God and the way His people had responded to it through the centuries. They weren't saying, *Now Jesus instead of all that*. No. They were saying, *See how Jesus encompassed and surpassed that grand, unchanging will of God that always was beautiful and desirable beyond words*. They were saying, *Now the Holy, which is no less holy, has come in human flesh, and He has given us the Holy Spirit to dwell within us*. What the people of God could not fathom before, got light years more unfathomable in the

Person of Jesus Christ and the Gift of the Holy Spirit. To ever, ever get casual about it, to reduce these supreme mysteries to something mundane and familiar, is a terrible desecration. Today's casual touching of the holy doesn't leave us dead on the spot, as in Old Testament days. Not physically, that is. But what deadness, what numbness of spirit is happening all around us as people casually touch the holy weekly, and daily? A theology of worship will intervene, and help to turn this terrible tide of our times.

The person and manner of Peter, Stephen, Paul was also encompassing. They didn't just appeal to one aspect of being. They weren't just trying to get the people to be logical or emotional or something else incomplete. Filled with the Holy Spirit, they were going for the hearts of their hearers; that is, the vital center of the whole being. Through signs, preaching, wonders, and teaching, they did reach hearts. When the people heard Stephen, "they were cut to the heart."[1] When they heard Peter, "they were pricked in their heart."[2] Encompassing men with an encompassing message reached hearts, and produced decisive results, for death or life. Refusing the message, the people killed Stephen; receiving Peter's message, they repented. There is an unmistakable power in that encompassing. Too often we are disappointed by lesser results. When that happens, we tend to emphasize one aspect or another. Even, sadly, we argue that one aspect or another is better: Reason is better than just devotion; or feeling is better than scholarship. But there must be a way to acknowledge our incompleteness and to move together toward the kind of encompassing Acts reveals. A theology of worship will help us do this.

In addition to being powerfully encompassing and presenting a powerfully encompassing message, the people of God in Acts also knew what was essential and stayed with it. It was essential that people, all people everywhere, encounter Jesus Christ—His life, death and resurrection—and know that He encompassed and surpassed all that God had previously done or desired for them. The people of God in Acts didn't deviate from this essential. This essential makes the whole book of Acts into a grand opening into worship. It also models a way for us to know and stay with what is essential in a theology of worship. There is a way to find and express what is essential in worship, and how encompassing and surpassing worship is. A

[1] Acts 7:54

[2] Acts 2:37

# Romans

The people of God in Old Testament times came to the house of God with a heartbreaking sense of what prevented them from entering into worship in the way their hearts, and God's heart, desired. They brought a living offering that would die as a result of their sin. With uncontrived humility they confessed their sin, and received God's forgiveness. Embraced by compassion, they were ready for worship.

In the book of Romans, Paul gives us the way to be reconciled to God by the death of his Son, Jesus Christ. This way encompasses and surpasses the heartbreaking experience of God's people through the centuries before. The Romans way is no less a matter of the heart than the way of God's Old Testament people. It is more so. The Romans way is no less vivid or real. It is more so. The Romans way involves no less humility, confession and forgiveness, and no less of God's compassion. The Romans way is God's eternal way culminating in the incarnation, death and resurrection of Jesus Christ.

The Romans way appeals to the foolish heart of the Gentile[1] and the impenitent heart of the Jew:[2] Repent, and believe in your heart. It is with the heart that we believe.[3] In our heart, that concentrated center of our being where every aspect of who we are is most keen, or potentially so—there it is that faith[4] is born, nurtured, and matured. Through a constantly maturing faith, our sight is restored, and our hearing, and our understanding. Each time I say, "O, now I see, and I realize there is even more to see," it is faith flexing in my soul. "O, now I hear, and know there is more to hear." "Now I understand, and want my understanding to increase." These are all faith flexing. By these faith calisthenics my heart wakes up, throws off its terrible lethargy, and through contrition and confession claims all the more of God's forgiveness and compassion. Embraced by God's forgiving compassion, and awed by His righteousness, I am where worship happens the way my heart and God's desire. A theology of worship will help us recognize the Romans way as the essential opening into worship that it is. $\mathcal{R}$

---

[1] Romans 1:21

[2] Romans 2:5

[3] Romans 10:9,10

[4] The Greek word *pistis* is translated as faith, belief, or trust. It takes at least three English words to convey, and draw us into, the power of *pistis*.

# 1 and 2 Corinthians

*You are a temple of God.[1] Your body is a temple of the Holy Spirit who is in you.[2] For we are the temple of the living God; just as God said, "I will dwell in them and walk among them; And I will be their God, and they shall be My people."[3]*

The whole Bible makes it clear that God wants to dwell among us and within us. The place and act of worship are always a response. What came first was God's desire to be with us. Tabernacle, sanctuary, temple, synagogue, church, house of God—each was intended to be a place of hospitality to the glory and goodness of God. Each is a place where holiness is received and responded to. Each is meant to be a place of worship. Before Paul said what he did to the Corinthians, this grand theme was already far beyond my ability to fully comprehend and live. Imagine, God wanting to be with us, and asking us to build a special place for this purpose! Receiving the presence of God was the whole reason they built those beautiful sanctuaries, the portable tabernacle in the desert and, later, the permanent temple. They built an immense amount of glory into these structures, but that glory produced by human hearts and hands was slight compared to the glory that filled the sanctuary as God entered. The glorious presence of God was visible and real to them. His holy presence was immeasurably dear to them, and this holiness also claimed their supreme respect: a holy fear of God.

Before I'm able to take in the wonders and the implications of God in His house on earth—for the sake of being with us—Paul

127

says, "You are a temple of God." How can I *ever*, how can any one of us or all of us together *ever* comprehend and live that! God is no less holy because His desire to be with His people brings Him not only into a house built for and dedicated to Him, not only among his people, but also into the very body of each of His people. I can never be soft and strong enough for the intimacy and immensity of this. Never, on my own. No wonder Paul also said, "No one can say, 'Jesus is Lord,' except by the Holy Spirit."[4] Just as I am not able to acknowledge Jesus as Lord without the Holy Spirit, neither am I able, on my own, to be soft and strong enough for the intimacy and immensity of being a temple of God.

My body, my life—the body and life of each Christian—becomes a place of hospitality to the glory and goodness of God. It becomes a place where holiness is received and responded to. Each Christian is a place of worship; gathered together, Christians are the church, a place where worship is even more than the sum of many worshippers. How do we ever receive and respond adequately to the holiness of God, either individually or together? What the Old Testament kept hidden inside the Holy of Holies is encompassed and surpassed in Jesus Christ. And each Christian becomes His temple. We need a great deal of help responding reverently to the intimacy and immensity of this. God is no less holy because Jesus Christ brings Him unthinkably close—into the very body of each of us. A theology of worship will show us how to be a temple of God, both individually and as a church. A theology of worship will help us be ever more aware of the holy, and always more reverent in response to it. *C*

---

[1] 1 Corinthians 3:16, NASB
[2] 1 Corinthians 6:19, NASB
[3] 2 Corinthians 6:16, NASB
[4] 1 Corinthians 12:3, NASB

# Galatians

Neither the Old Testament nor the New Testament people of God approached worship casually. What the Old Testament taught about the heart-changing approach to worship was magnified in the New Testament. At the Old Testament altar, a person approaching worship would see sin and its consequences with heartbreaking clarity. Through confession and forgiveness the sinner is reunited with God and experiences His compassion. Then, with deep sadness and equally deep joy, the forgiven Old Testament sinner entered into worship.

In the New Testament it is still so; no, it is *more* so. The New Testament people of God don't approach worship casually either. Approaching worship, the New Testament child of God sees sin and its consequences at Calvary with heartbreaking clarity, and is crucified with Christ.[1] Then, with deep sadness and equally deep joy, the forgiven New Testament sinner enters into worship.

This all happens through the calisthenics of the heart known as *pistis* (faith, trust, or belief). A theology of worship will show us the genuine and heart-full way of pistis. It is a way with a royal vision of the indescribable goodness of God known as righteousness.[2] So many beautiful perfections attract us to God. Each perfection—such as mercy, justice, compassion, and power—is full of wonder. When they are all combined the result surpasses any beauty or perfection we can imagine. This surpassing combination is called righteousness. Righteousness is the infinitely attractive and utterly unattainable expression of God's being. This righteousness is the vision of *pistis*.

This is its guiding star. By righteousness, *pistis* revives no matter what; because of righteousness, *pistis* survives any circumstances. Righteousness compels and completes *pistis*, and frees *pistis* to be all that it was ever meant to be. Because righteousness *is*, *pistis* waits with contentment, fights with courage, hopes steadfastly, and through all, it longs with inexpressible love. Righteousness is the morning sun and the evening rest of *pistis*; and forever its renewable hunger. Through *pistis*, the New Testament sinner continually reaches new depths of grief and joy in the Cross and Resurrection. 𝒢

[1] Galatians 2:16,20; 5:24; 6:14

[2] Galatians 5:5

# Ephesians

Ephesians contains a grand and sustaining prayer. The heights
and the hopes in this prayer make the humble work of discipline
and doctrine all worthwhile. It is humble work to struggle through
doctrinal and discipline issues. Much of this must not have seemed
inspiring or rewarding for those involved. Yet a prayer like the one
in Ephesians 3:14-21 puts it all in perspective. This is what it's about.
This is why each of those doctrinal and discipline issues is important.

*For this reason I kneel before the Father, from whom his whole
family in heaven and on earth derives its name. I pray that
out of his glorious riches he may strengthen you with power
through his Spirit in your inner being, so that Christ may dwell
in your hearts through faith. And I pray that you, being rooted
and established in love, may have power, together with all the
saints, to grasp how wide and long and high and deep is the love
of Christ, and to know this love that surpasses knowledge —that
you may be filled to the measure of all the fullness of God.*

*Now to him who is able to do immeasurably more than all we
ask or imagine, according to his power that is at work within us,
to him be glory in the church and in Christ Jesus throughout all
generations, for ever and ever! Amen.* [1]

This prayer—planted in the heart of Ephesians, and in the heart
of each Christian who has ever read and loved Ephesians—is a grand
opening into worship.

- God's glorious riches
- Strength
- Power
- God's Spirit
- Our inner being
- Christ dwelling in our heart
- Faith

Each of these is packed into one sentence. What a sentence![2] It tells about the Spirit of God strengthening and empowering us so Christ can dwell in our hearts by that life-giving *pistis* response. In Old Testament times, through the most careful preparation, a tabernacle or temple became a sanctuary where God actually did dwell. It became a place of the most reverent encounter with the Holy.

In New Testament times a human heart becomes the dwelling place of Christ and therefore a place of worship. Is God any less holy when He dwells in a human heart? Is our encounter with God meant to be any less reverent than the Old Testament people of God experienced? Is a New Testament child of God meant to prepare the tabernacle of the heart with any less care or attention to detail than the Old Testament people of God used in preparing God's house? What *is* involved in preparing our hearts to be the dwelling place of Christ and therefore a place of worship? A theology of worship will help us ponder and live into these things. A theology of worship will show us how *pistis* draws us into worship that is always more grand, more reverent, and more full of heart and wonder.

The Ephesians prayer ends this way:

*Now to him who is able to do immeasurably more than all we ask or imagine, according to his power that is at work within us, to him be glory in the church and in Christ Jesus throughout all generations, for ever and ever! Amen.[3]*

Near the time of his death, Jesus prayed, "Now my heart is troubled, and what shall I say? 'Father, save me from this hour'? No, it was for this very reason I came to this hour. Father, glorify your name!"[4]

"Then a voice came from heaven, 'I have glorified it, and will glorify it again.'"[5]

By the end of Ephesians we know Christ and His Church are the means of answering the prayer: Father, glorify your name! Christ and His Church answer this prayer. Ephesians presents them both, not individual and separate, but married. We get caught up in figuring out whether Paul was equitable enough in what he said about husbands and wives, and miss out on the larger, richer and surpassing beauty of what he was saying:

*This is a great mystery: but I speak concerning Christ and the church.*

What a beloved, unimaginable mystery that Christ and His church are united and love each other as they do. The best we can imagine of the best marriage can introduce us to this mystery of the union between Christ and His church.

Is the church a place of worship? Was it meant to be? What foolish, foolish questions. Christ dwells and is worshipped in the heart of each *pistis*-filled member. When these individual worshippers gather, what happens? What is meant to happen? How does all that individual worship combine, harmonize, and surpass the worship of individuals? How does this worship in the church that is united with Christ in the dearest of all loves, how does this worship encompass and surpass all the reverence, all the holy fear, all the glory of all the worship introduced so far throughout all the Bible, throughout all the history of God's people on earth? A theology of worship has so much to tell us, so much to show us. A theology of worship will guide our hearts into the fullness of worship. ☖

---

[1] Ephesians 3:14-21, NIV
[2] Actually, in the KJV all of Ephesians 3:14-19 is one sentence!
[3] Ephesians 3:20-21, NIV
[4] John 12:27-28a, NIV
[5] John 12:28b, NIV

# <u>Philippians</u>

Christ dwells in human hearts and by His indwelling makes them a place of worship. Christ also dwells among human hearts in His church, the Love of His Life! Worship fills the hearts of individuals and worship fills his church. Worship extends even beyond that.

Here's how Paul describes the incredible expansion of worship:

*Who [Christ Jesus], being in very nature God,*
  *did not consider equality with God something to be grasped,*
*but made himself nothing,*
  *taking the very nature of a servant,*
  *being made in human likeness.*
*And being found in appearance as a man,*
  *he humbled himself*
  *and became obedient to death — even death on a cross!*
*Therefore God exalted him to the highest place*
  *and gave him the name that is above every name,*
*that at the name of Jesus every knee should bow,*
  *in heaven and on earth and under the earth,*
*and every tongue confess that Jesus Christ is Lord,*
  *to the glory of God the Father.* [1]

Everyone, everywhere on earth, under the earth, and in heaven — everywhere — everyone will bow and worship and confess that Jesus Christ is Lord, to the glory of God the Father. All worship, individual and corporate, contributes to and prepares us for that grand, unanimous worship.

Is there any reason we would not see that day as something to prepare for, even more than (for example) a choir rehearses? The more the choir hopes to be inspired and to inspire, the more the choir rehearses. Is there any reason for us to put less into preparing our whole being (not just our voices) for the Grand Day of Unanimous Worship in the entire universe? Is there any reason we would not participate in that worship now as often and as much as possible? A theology of worship will show us the way to prepare for the Grand Day of Unanimous Worship, and it will show us how to participate in that Grand Day even now, today.

Humbling myself and becoming obedient to death, the kind of dying that happened on the Cross, I can expect these to be involved in worship, just as they were involved for the One who receives my worship. A theology of worship will faithfully show us the connection between humility, obedience to death, death on the Cross, the connection between these and the worship we prepare for and participate in today. ℘

---

[1] Philippians 2:6-11, NIV

# *Colossians*

As I let three versions of Colossians 2:2-3, and two introductions to the book of Colossians settle in, this is what I hear. Deeply aware of their sin, the Colossians were trying to achieve perfection in ways that were some mix of legalistic and ascetic. They were turning to Judaism, speculative philosophy and a host of angelic mediators. As a result, they seemed to be receiving some sense of superior wisdom and insight into the mysteries of the universe, if not freedom from their craving for sanctification.

Paul struggles for them and for those at Laodicea. It was the kind of struggle a heart knows when desiring and doing the best for loved ones who don't yet value the gift. What he hoped to accomplish by this struggle included comforting their hearts.[1] He knew they would be comforted by assurance, *full* assurance that they understood enough (that they were in fact *rich* in understanding) of what they really needed.[2] They needed to know the mystery of God, namely, Christ, in whom are hidden all the treasures of wisdom and knowledge.[3]

Christ the One Essential and Ultimate Mystery is all and in all.[4] "We have redemption through his blood, even the forgiveness of sins." "For by him were all things created, that are in heaven, and that are in earth, visible and invisible, whether they be thrones, or dominions, or principalities, or powers: all things were created by him, and for him: And he is before all things, and by him all things consist. And he is the head of the body, the church: who is the beginning, the firstborn from the dead; that in all things he might have the preeminence."[5]

In this One Essential and Ultimate Mystery are hidden all the treasures of wisdom and knowledge.

> *Oh, the depth of the riches of the wisdom and knowledge of God!*
> *How unsearchable his judgments, and his paths beyond tracing out!*
> *Who has known the mind of the Lord?*
> *Or who has been his counselor?*
> *Who has ever given to God, that God should repay him?*
> *For from him and through him and to him are all things.*
> *To him be the glory forever! Amen.*[6]

This One Essential and Ultimate Mystery is humble and accessible beyond belief, and also so far past our full comprehension! How can we ever take in His humble mercy *and also* His overwhelming, holy power? A theology of worship will help us claim the hope and comfort of his humble accessibility at the same time that it prepares us to stand back in awe of his holy power. A theology of worship will assure us that we can know enough; it will also spare us from oversimplifying. It will show us how to befriend and respect the One Essential and Ultimate Mystery. *C*

---

[1] Colossians 2:1-2, KJV and NIV
[2] Colossians 2:2, NASB and NIV
[3] Colossians 2:2-3, NIV
[4] Colossians 3:11
[5] Colossians 1:14,16-18
[6] Romans 11:33-36, NIV

# 1 and 2 Thessalonians

First and Second Thessalonians are probably the earliest preserved letters from Paul. In about A.D. 50, people in Thessalonica had turned from idols to serve the living and true God; and to wait for his Son from heaven, whom he raised from the dead, even Jesus.[1] Composed of mostly Gentiles, this church suffered persecution like the churches in Judea suffered.[2] The two letters from Paul to the Thessalonian believers are full of affection, comfort, anticipation of the Second Coming of Jesus, and correction and instruction.

These Thessalonians believed and lived the gospel. They were called into the kingdom and glory of God.[3] Paul commended their work of faith, labor of love, and patience of hope in our Lord Jesus Christ.[4] With exemplary faith, love and hope they responded to the death, resurrection and anticipated Second Coming of Jesus.[5] What a grand span of time and events they were responding to! It is the same span from first to second advent that we live in today. They, of course, were close to His first coming; we are much closer to His second coming. What does worship have to do with living between the first and second advents of Jesus? The books of Hebrews and Revelation will contribute magnificently in response to that question! Meanwhile the letters to the Thessalonians open into worship with words like these:

*For the Lord himself shall descend from heaven with a shout, with the voice of the archangel, and with the trump of God.[6]*

When this happens, will we worship? Shouldn't the question be, could we imagine *not* worshipping when this happens? Does anticipation of this moment involve and affect our worship today? A theology of worship will reflect on these things as it shows us the way of worship between the first and second advents of Jesus. ⟨

[1] 1 Thessalonians 1:8,9

[2] 1 Thessalonians 2:14,15

[3] 1 Thessalonians 2:12

[4] 1 Thessalonians 2:13 and 1:3

[5] The Second Coming of Jesus is mentioned in 1 Thessalonians 1:10; 2:19; 3:13; 4:16-17; 5:2,23 and 2 Thessalonians 1:7ff; 2:2,8; 3:5

[6] 1 Thessalonians 4:16

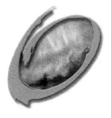

# 1 and 2 Timothy

"Pursue righteousness."[1] Paul told Timothy to pursue righteousness.

Righteousness and *pistis* have a special relationship, an endearing connection, that helps a person do what Paul said.

Righteousness is not a matter of indifference to *pistis*! Nor is it a theory or an abstraction. Righteousness is the vision and hope of *pistis*. *Pistis* is deeply indebted to righteousness, and knows it. Righteousness gives *pistis* deep, lasting joy. Neither righteousness nor *pistis* is an abstraction; they are each embodied. Righteousness is summed up in Jesus Christ, and *pistis* expresses itself in each of His followers.

Whenever we give much time, attention, energy and commitment — in a word, deep and lasting love — to pursuing something that matters to us, we are sampling what it means to pursue righteousness. When we admire, are "taken with," "given to," and immersed in something, that's a small taste of what it means to pursue righteousness. Righteousness could be called the *Love* of Faith's life! This is so because righteousness sums up the character of The One Who is All and in All for *pistis*. In pursuit of righteousness, *pistis* becomes radical, but not fanatical. Everything good serves the pursuit of righteousness. Sound doctrines are each a stepping-stone on the way to righteousness. Sound doctrines, so vitally important in the pastoral epistles, give clarity and grounding to righteousness; and none confines, obscures or restricts it. The Word of Truth, the holy and inspired Scriptures,[2] serves the endearing connection between *pistis* and righteousness. Virtues, such as patience and meekness, strengthen and sustain *pistis* in its pursuit of righteousness.

Strengthened by the love of righteousness, *pistis* confesses and conquers sin and endures suffering. Detours, defeats, sidetracks, and disappointments slow or sadden *pistis*; but they don't stop it. *Pistis* is sustained by its endearing, life-giving connection with righteousness.

A young minister such as Timothy or Titus who pursues righteousness will encounter Jesus Christ over and over. It's unavoidable! These encounters with Jesus, the Personification of Righteousness, will not remain theoretical. They will not remain distant. They will not focus only on Jesus' humanity. The young minister pursuing righteousness will encounter Jesus' divinity also, and in that encounter discover riches in worship that will never be exhausted in this life or in eternity. A theology of worship will show us all (not just ministers) the endearing connection between *pistis* and righteousness. It will show us how to pursue righteousness all the way into worship. *T*

---

[1] 1 Timothy 6:11, NASB and NIV
[2] 1 Timothy 2:15; 3:15-16

# Titus

*Looking for that blessed hope, and the glorious appearing of the great God and our Saviour Jesus Christ.*[1]

In many ways, and on most every page, the New Testament talks about the glorious Second Coming of Christ. Tucked away in this tiny letter to Titus are some of the best-known and loved of the many New Testament accounts of this glorious event. These words of Paul to Titus (and to all Christians) have always been words to live by and die by; words to cherish. The hope and power of them grow and grow—like the light that shines more and more unto the perfect day.[2]

It is our heritage as Christians to anticipate the Second Coming of Christ. We are called to do this with the uncontrived and buoyant eagerness of a child and also the enduring and seasoned faith of maturity.[3]

In addition to being loved and longed for as intended, the Second Coming of Christ has also been feared, assumed, compromised, and avoided in many ways. We may not always find the hope blessed, we don't always respond ideally. But we have felt the desired response. Perhaps during an inspiring sermon, or when hearing a grand hymn about His Coming, or when in personal communion with God, the glorious coming of Christ becomes real to our hearts. Yet we want, and need, more than occasional highs about Christ's Glorious Coming; we need to do more than feel good about it, and then let it fall back into the shadows of our life as a favorite assumption.

When Christ came as an infant, His people were loving and

longing for His Coming. Two examples of this are Simeon and Anna. Simeon was waiting, looking, for the consolation of Israel. Anna, who never left the temple but worshiped night and day, gave thanks to God and spoke about the child to all who were looking forward to the redemption of Jerusalem.[4] It's Simeon and Anna, especially Anna, who speak to me of the kind of anticipation for His Glorious Coming that my heart longs for.

Her anticipation was bound together with worship. Worship was anticipation. This is dear to my heart, my heart that is reaching for fuller realization of it. A theology of worship will show me, will show us, the way to worship as anticipation of Christ's Glorious Coming. This anticipation is expanded and strengthened night and day in worship. This is, in fact, an arduous way, but a deeply significant, soul-satisfying way to prepare for the grandest culmination of worship at Christ's Glorious Coming. A theology of worship will lead us into the ardor, the humility and the hope of worshipful anticipating of the Blessed Hope and Glorious Appearing of our Savior Jesus Christ. *T*

[1] Titus 2:13

[2] Proverbs 4:18

[3] Matthew 18:3; Titus 2:2

[4] Luke 2:25,37-38

# Philemon

Worship and worshippers go together. How are worshippers meant to relate? In response to that question, we can ponder the experience of Onesimus, Philemon and Paul. Paul's letter is written to the church in Philemon's house, as well as to Philemon. When distance or some other circumstance prevented them from worshipping at the house of God, the Old Testament people of God built an altar. When circumstances prevented them from worshipping in the house of God, New Testament people of God had church in their house.

There may be more parallels than we have noticed between those Old Testament altars and the New Testament house churches. One parallel that seems especially valuable to notice in the experience of Onesimus, Philemon and Paul is what happened at the altar and later in New Testament house churches. At the altar, sin was humbly recognized and confessed, and the compassion of God was received. This happened in the most heartfelt ways. Humility, the confession of sin, the compassion of God, each sank deep into the being of the worshipper. This mingling of humility, confession and the compassion of God opened the door into the worship that followed.

What an account of this mingling is given to us in the letter to Philemon! For Onesimus, Philemon and Paul, individually, this mingling of humility, confession and the compassion of God must have been deeply significant; when the experience of the three men combined into community, the significance expanded, so much that it's still touching our lives today.

The power and tenderness these worshippers experienced is

emphasized by three uses of the Greek word *splagchna* in Philemon. *Splagchna* is only used in six other places in the Bible. It's a word that seems odd or embarrassing to some of us when it's translated as bowels. And yet, anyone who's ever had their "stomach growl" very loudly and inconveniently is prepared to understand that deep feelings (as well as hunger or indigestion!) are registered in the bowels. Paul felt deeply and intensely about the circumstance that he, along with Onesimus and Philemon, was going through. In feeling that deeply, and expressing his feelings, Paul shows us an indispensable dimension of life among worshippers. A theology of worship will help us claim and integrate this dimension. It will help us enter all the more fully into worship that is served by, and filled with, the deepest feeling. $\mathcal{P}$

# Hebrews

*Now of the things which we have spoken this is the sum: We have such an high priest, who is set on the right hand of the throne of the Majesty in the heavens; A minister of the sanctuary, and of the true tabernacle, which the Lord pitched, and not man.[1]*

Our high priest is introduced this way in the first chapter of Hebrews:

*In the past God spoke to our forefathers through the prophets at many times and in various ways, but in these last days he has spoken to us by his Son, whom he appointed heir of all things, and through whom he made the universe. The Son is the radiance of God's glory and the exact representation of his being, sustaining all things by his powerful word. After he had provided purification for sins, he sat down at the right hand of the Majesty in heaven. So he became as much superior to the angels as the name he has inherited is superior to theirs.*

*For to which of the angels did God ever say,*
*"You are my Son;*
*today I have become your Father"?*
*Or again,*
*"I will be his Father,*
*and he will be my Son"?*
*And again, when God brings his firstborn into the world, he says,*
*"Let all God's angels worship him."[2]*

Hebrews shows that Old Testament worship has been transfigured. All the goodness, all the heart, all the reverence, all the blessing God always meant for His people to experience in worship is encompassed and surpassed now that the Creator and Redeemer reigns and ministers in the heavenly sanctuary.

Old Testament worship as God intended it was deeply significant and full of hope, and it all led into the glorious worship that Hebrews unfurls. Old Testament worship was glorious and New Testament worship infinitely surpasses it. Worshippers—the people of God—are to follow from glory to infinitely surpassing glory. Their sense of the holy and their reverent response is to increase in magnitude as the glory does. What heart-yearning that creates! Will I, will we, ever approach the glory with the sense of the holy and the reverence—the holy fear—it receives from those who are close to it. Why would I, why would we, stay blind, casual or indifferent to a glory so compelling? A theology of worship will mercifully sensitize us to the magnitude of worship, and to its claims in our life individually and as His church. It will show us how to follow the yearning of our heart for entering into the surpassing worship Hebrews calls for.

At the moment I am writing this, and at the moment you are reading this, Jesus reigns and ministers in the heavenly sanctuary. We look to him.[3] We come to the city of the living God, the heavenly Jerusalem.[4] By him we praise God continually, giving thanks to his name.[5]

When we come to New Testament worship, we will span the distance from earth to heaven. Worship is not earth-based any more.[6] Jesus reigns and ministers in the heavenly sanctuary, and we are to follow him there. *Pistis* was never more crucial, and never more challenged. No wonder there's a whole chapter in Hebrews about incredible feats of faith! New Testament worship is an ultimate feat of faith, and those Hebrews 11 examples encourage us to persevere. *H*

---

[1] Hebrews 8:1-2. See also Hebrews 9:24.

[2] Hebrews 1:1-6, NIV

[3] Hebrews 12:2

[4] Hebrews 12:22

[5] Hebrews 13:15

[6] Though some Old Testament people of God, like the Psalmists, knew it really never was entirely earth-based. See Psalms 11:4; 18:6,9,13; 68:32-33; 89:5-8; and Psalm 97, NIV.

# James

*Draw near to God and He will draw near to you.*[1]

From the prodigal son story, I gratefully anticipate God's heart and arms open with compassion and love when I draw near. From great hymns of faith I know to expect safety and rest when I draw near to God: "There is a place of quiet rest, near to the heart of God."[2] Compassion, comfort, and merrymaking happen when we draw near to God. It is so good. So inviting.

And there is even more. Worship will be another, and more ultimate, soul-satisfying consequence of doing as James said. When merciful rays of God's glory break through the sheltering veil between us; when my heart is healing and my eyes opening, then, as I draw near to Him I am not only comforted by His compassion; I worship. Approaching God is always an approach to holiness, and in His mercy that approach will reduce me to the unspeakable joy of worship.

A theology of worship will show us the approach to God's holiness; it will teach us to seek and receive His mercy; it will show us the way to have our heart healed and our eyes opened; it will prepare us to be reduced to the unspeakable joy of worship.

James said several things that are involved in this preparation. He said to be patient. He said we need "long patience,"[3] that we need the early and latter rain. He said to humble ourselves in the sight of the Lord.[4] He said to be impartial and compassionate and to visit the fatherless and widows.[5] He said to purify[6] and strengthen our hearts.[7] James also pointed us to the timeless truth of the central place of God's Law. James may well have shared the Psalmist's love of God's law, the love of and delight in God's Law that introduce all the Psalms, Psalm 1:2, and that fill the longest of them, Psalm 119. This love for and joy in the law is an expression of the heart and it is positioned in the heart of the Bible. The Law of God on the tables of stone was positioned inside the Ark of the Covenant at the heart of Israel's worship. Over and over the Old Testament repeats the same timeless truth: the law of God and loving that law with a heart free of legalism is at the heart of worship. A theology of worship will show us the way to keep the Law of God at the heart of worship as a matter of the heart.

---

[1] James 4:8, NASB

[2] First line of the hymn titled *Near to the Heart of God*, words and tune by Cleland B. McAfee (1866-1944).

[3] James 5:7

[4] James 4:10

[5] James 1:27; 2:3-4. See also Psalm 68 where worship and compassion for the poor are bound together. In addition to clothing and food, and in an even more foundational way, the destitute need what worship gives them. They need worship because of how it assures them of the overarching and ever-present power and love of God, and they also need worship because of how it equalizes them with other worshippers—rich and poor—all of whom are utterly fragile and small compared to God. In worship, nobody, rich or poor, focuses on money the way they do without worship. James 2:15-16 combined with Psalm 68 opens not only into worship that is full of compassion, but also into compassion that is full of worship. Compassion that is full of worship makes the difference between secular social service and the Gospel.

[6] James 4:8

[7] James 5:8, NASB

# 1 and 2 Peter

*But grow in grace, and in the knowledge of our Lord and Saviour Jesus Christ. To him be glory both now and for ever. Amen.*[1]

These words end the second epistle of Peter, and they sum up both epistles. The beginning of the second letter tells how grace and peace are multiplied to us through the knowledge of God and of Jesus our Lord. Divine power, through magnificent and precious promises makes us partakers of the divine nature. We progress from faith through virtue, knowledge, self-control, patience, godliness, and kindness to love. When these things are in us, and increasing, then our knowledge of Jesus is alive and fruitful.

The epistles of Peter reveal the grand sweep of the power and glory of Jesus from his suffering and death through his resurrection on to his glorious Second Coming and beyond that to the new heavens and new earth. We take in—receive and realize—this power and glory through the ever-increasing faith-to-love progression.

This growing and increasing in the knowledge of Jesus opens us into worship. That's where the faith-to-love progression in response to the cross-to-new earth glory takes us! A theology of worship will keep that connection clear. A theology of worship won't let us just focus on being nice, well-behaved Christians. It will keep us immersed in the worship-inspiring glory of Jesus from the cross to the new earth. It will show us how the faith-to-love progression prepares us for worship, and how the same progression becomes worship.

To him be glory and dominion for ever and ever. Amen.[2] A theology of worship will give us this doxology of Peter's, and show us how to love and live it more every day. $\mathcal{P}$

---

[1] 2 Peter 3:18
[2] 1 Peter 5:11

# 1, 2 and 3 John

Positioned as they are in the Bible, the three John epistles (and Jude) become like a doorway into Revelation. The three brief John epistles address issues of their time. In the process, they emphasized the incarnation, confession of sin, and the return of Jesus. Each of these is an opening into worship, as it is a transforming reality in the life of God's people. Together the incarnation, confession of sin, and the return of Jesus become a kind of passport into the grandeur of Revelation.

Each of these transforming realities is grounded in love, and tested, expressed, and purified by love. This love comes from God who is Love.

*Beloved, let us love one another, for love is from God; and everyone who loves is born of God and knows God. The one who does not love does not know God, for God is love.*[1]

God is love. Knowing God is the crucial key to love. How much, how long, how well we know God determines how much, how long, and how well we love.

*We know God because*
*we see Jesus in action*
*we hear Jesus' words*
*we think about what Jesus said and did*
*and who He was;*
*we ponder.*

*More than that, we know God because*
*we take Jesus into our very being,*
*into our Heart.*
 *This brings us to silent reverence in His presence.*
 *It brings us to worship.*

Reverent worship is love's fullest expression. Reverent worship is what happens when we realize that the One we love really is God. Worship is love transposed—exponentially!

*In worship we love with a love*
 *that is as full of holy fear*
 *as it is of intimacy.*
*In worship we know the King of all*
 *as Royal Ruler*
 *not just as friend*
 *or problem solver.*
*Worship magnifies*
 *holy fear*
 *as it also magnifies*
  *the most cherished and holy intimacy.*

A theology of worship will show us the way to love transposed into worship. It will take us through John's door into worship's fullness. ⌋

---

¹ 1 John 4:7-8, NASB

# *Jude*

By *pistis*, our hearts lay claim to righteousness; love, the greatest
of all the powers of our being, transposes into worship. Jude focuses
on this as he ends his letter urging his much-loved readers to be in
the process of building themselves up through their most holy faith
and praying in the Holy Spirit as they keep themselves in the love of
God. *Pistis*, Spirit and love are what they are to concern themselves
with as they are looking for the mercy of our Lord Jesus Christ
unto eternal life. And, as they anticipate receiving mercy, they are to
extend mercy, with compassion or fear as the case indicates.[1]

In the next breath Jude ends with this doxology:

> *To him who is able to keep you from falling and to present you
> before his glorious presence without fault and with great joy—to
> the only God our Savior be glory, majesty, power and authority,
> through Jesus Christ our Lord, before all ages, now and forever-
> more! Amen.*[2]

The glory, majesty, power and authority of God through Jesus
Christ our Lord—forevermore—is what everything moves toward.
It is also the starting-point and reason for everything. Jude's beloved
were threatened by the most treacherous and disgusting deceivers
who were clouds without water, trees without fruit, twice dead; rag-
ing waves foaming out their own shame; wandering stars, to whom
is reserved the blackness of darkness for ever. But these people (that
Jude exposes with choice words!) were subject to the surpassing
power of God that is glimpsed in the words of the doxology. By this

doxology, Jude returns his endangered readers to their sustaining power, to their supreme comfort and hope.

What rich territory this is for a theology of worship, especially positioned where it is as the last step before entering the book of Revelation! Building ourselves up in *pistis*, and keeping ourselves in God's love, involve praying in the Spirit. This vitality, this strengthening and deepening of *pistis* and love through communion with God are the groundwork of worship. They are foundations to doxology. How do people come to the place where Jude's doxology is the uncontrived expression of their own heart? Through the kind of communion with God that builds us up in *pistis* and keeps us in the love of God. A theology of worship will show us the essential connection between that kind of individual communion with God and the congregation's worship.

A theology of worship will also show us how each congregation that has ever worshipped God—imagine how many, through the centuries!—each participates in and yet only anticipates the grand, unimaginably grand, culmination of worship portrayed in Revelation. ⫛

[1] Jude 20-23, NASB
[2] Jude 24-25, NIV

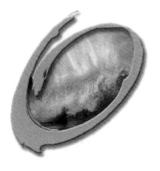

# Revelation

People of God ponder, puzzle and pray over the book of Revelation. Then they preach it. And some practice it.

If it were possible to portray on an Imax screen what John describes in Revelation, it would be the ultimate media production of all time. But the earth-and-heaven-encompassing magnitude of Revelation can't be contained by any or all media power or by any or all of the power of human minds.

Revelation doesn't reduce to sermons or movies. Though in the mercy of God, we can be blessed by humble human attempts to cooperate with the Spirit in making this grand book known.

Living its happenings is the ultimate way to know the book of Revelation. The people of God, and their enemies, have done this and will do this. Doing so carries God's people through the extremes of threat, persecution and suffering and into indescribably sublime worship. This worship culminates in such an encompassing and resounding way:

*Who will not fear you, O Lord,*
*and bring glory to your name?*
*For you alone are holy.*
*All nations will come*
*and worship before you.*[1]

*I heard what sounded like the roar of a great multitude... like*
*the roar of rushing waters and like loud peals of thunder,*
*shouting:*

*Hallelujah!*
  *For our Lord God Almighty reigns.*
  *Let us rejoice and be glad*
  *And give him glory![2]*

Worship rolls through heaven and earth, something like, but infinitely better than, the sound of thunder and roaring waters. All nations on earth and all creatures in Heaven worship God. Eventually everyone everywhere in all time and eternity worships God. In numerous places throughout the book of Revelation, this worship is expressed with soul-stretching, God-glorifying words.

In addition to being a grand and ultimate climax to come, worship is a very present companion that sustains and comforts God's people in the midst of everything. "Worthy is the Lamb that was slain to receive power and riches and wisdom and strength and honour and glory and blessing"[3] is today's reality, not just tomorrow's promise. God's people worship the Lamb now. *Worship God* is, in fact, their mandate.[4]

Revelation is the grand finale of the Bible, and its worship is the grand finale of worship. With soul-stirring splendor, worship spans earth and heaven, time and eternity. The sounds of it surpass anything we have ever heard; the heart of it expresses more than we have begun to imagine. The joy of it is far beyond our comprehension.

Actually worship is even more than grand finale. It is the great *therefore* of Scripture. *Therefore* sums up all that precedes it, and sends us forth into what follows. Worship sums up our response to God and sends us forth into new heights and depths in response to God's limitless holy love and power. We will never in all eternity stop finding new causes for worship.

A theology of worship will help us claim, love, and live this heritage of worship—today. It will prepare us to do this all the more at the glorious Second Coming of Jesus. It will show us worship that is not earth-bound, not even today. It will show us the glorified Jesus in the midst of the seven candlesticks, as well as the sandal-clad Jesus in Nazareth. It will show us the holy fear[5] we need to have in order to worship. It will condition our hearts to receive and respond to the One who is divine as well as human. It will comfort our hearts that when earth and heaven are new, the tabernacle of God will be with us and he will dwell with us, and we will be God's people; God himself will be with us, and be our God.[6] The same God who said, "Let them make me a sanctuary that I may dwell among them,"[7] the same God who tabernacled among us in the person of Jesus Christ,[8] this same God will do what His heart has always, always wanted. He will tabernacle among us, and we will worship! It is so good. So very good. ℛ

[1] Revelation 15:4, NIV

[2] Revelation 19:1,6,7, NIV

[3] Revelation 5:12

[4] Revelation 14:7

[5] Revelation 14:7

[6] Revelation 21:1-3

[7] Exodus 25:8

[8] John 1:14, NASB margin

# Afterword

I've been asked what this book has done for me. If you should wonder that also, I want you to know that this book assures my heart of precious things. Some of these assurances already had a history with me, and this book has strengthened and beautified them. New assurances are added to them. Having them all together in one place strengthens and beautifies all of them.

- *Worship is a pervasive and grand theme through the whole Bible. Every book of the Bible opens into worship.*

- *Worship is central, compelling and over-arching in the life of God's people, both when they are alone and when they are together.*

- *Worship involves hospitality where according to God's specifications we create a protected place, a sanctuary, where God dwells.*

- *Worship connects heaven and earth, today and at the Second Coming of Jesus.*

- *Worship inspires, and requires, a keen and ever-developing sense of the holy, and ever-deepening reverence, which is also known as holy fear.*

- *The New Testament encompasses and surpasses the timeless Old Testament truths about worship.*

- *Worship can't be contrived or staged, and it isn't a production or a performance.*

- *Worship takes us beyond ourselves and into the glory of God. In such worship, love is transposed and transfigured and the result is a truly indescribable level and quality of joy.*

- *An adequate theology of worship is impossible to express, much less live; yet worship is our heritage. We can receive this heritage and love and live it more fully each day.*

- *There are essentials to worship that are like the foundations of a building or the roots of a tree. These are common to all God's people. They steady and support us as we find our way through diversity.*

- *A theology of worship is something to which every prayerful worshipper can contribute. This can happen in various ways as individuals and groups discover what to include and then share this with each other, and with those prepared to articulate it for the church.*

- *Seeking God with our whole heart, communion with God, every Spirit-led way of knowing God, all of these serve worship. The quality and depth of our communion with God will shape our experience of worship.*

- *Worship is an especially fitting emphasis among people who anticipate the glorious Second Coming of Jesus. What worship that will be! All worship now prepares us for that worship and for the eternity of worship to follow. Joining in with those who always say, "Holy, Holy, Holy," will be our indescribable joy forever.*

- *Law (never legalism), obedience, sound doctrine and service all complement worship. Worship isn't complete without them, and they are not complete without worship. For example, to give food to the hungry and not worship, is to sadly miss the deepest need of their being, just as giving them worship without food is to deny the obvious need of their body.*

- *Even when I am still far from being the worshipper I want to become, I have the gift of longing for worship. I cherish this longing as the dawn into the full day of worship.*

There's something else this book is doing for me. It gives me a way to share these assurances with you, the reader. It gives me a way to say, please receive, love, and live these assurances for yourself. I hope the assurances will be contagious, and that they will contribute to always more reverent and meaningful worship for individuals and congregations.

# You can benefit from this book in a number of ways.

- You can read it and reflect however you reflect on such reading.

- You can respond to the comments and questions about a theology of worship that are in each section of the book. Using these comments and questions, you can pray and ponder your way toward a theology of worship. You might share your results, and in that way contribute to a more complete theology of worship in your local church, and beyond.

- You may choose to start where I did, and move through the Bible discovering how each book of the Bible opens into worship for you. Several books similar to this one, by a variety of authors, will make a theology of worship all the more complete!

However you choose to benefit from this book, know that it is sent into the church and the world consecrated to God, and it is sent with daily prayers that it will have and give the life God wants it to have and give.